W9-BUY-367

Falling into Greatness

by
Lloyd John Ogilvie

THOMAS NELSON PUBLISHERS
Nashville · Camden · New York

Published in Nashville, Tennessee, by Thomas Nelson, Inc. and distributed in Canada by Lawson Falle, Ltd., Cambridge, Ontario.

Printed in the United States of America.

The Scripture text in this publication is from THE NEW KING JAMES VERSION. Copyright © 1979, 1980, 1982, Thomas Nelson, Inc., Publishers.

Library of Congress Cataloging in Publication Data

Ogilvie, Lloyd John.
  Falling into greatness.

  1. Bible. O.T. Psalms—Criticism, interpretation, etc. 2. Christian life—Presbyterian authors. I. Title.
BS1430.2.036   1984   223′.206   84-1946
ISBN 0-8407-5326-8

To Commander G.H.L. Kitson, O.B.E. R.N. (Ret.) and his lovely wife, Betty, beloved friends through the years, for the greatness through the Lord's grace they exemplify in their commitment to Him, their leadership in extending His kingdom, their enthusiasm for living life as an adventure, their love for people, and their ability to encourage and enable greatness in others.

Contents

Introduction

In our fast-track race through life, problems trip us. We stumble and fall.

This book is about how to fall into greatness. The words seem contradictory at first. Falling into greatness? How can any failure be an opportunity for growth in greatness? The secret is in discovering how to fall into the greatness of God.

He is ready to catch us when we fall. When we are caught by His everlasting arms, we discover His true greatness. We experience His grace—unchanging, unqualified, unlimited love. If we never fail, we miss the reliability of His gracious arm. But Jehovah-Shammah, "the Lord is there," is always present to turn our discouragements into deeper discoveries of our own potential greatness through Him. His grace, multiplied by our gratitude, equals greatness.

That greatness grows when we are honest with God about our difficulties in our relationships and responsibilities. Inside all of us is an inner world of thought and feeling. In this private world, we talk to ourselves, reflect on what's happening to and around us, and mull over our deepest hurts and hopes. Far too seldom do we feel secure enough with others to open our inner self to them. We project an image of adequacy and sufficiency. What they see often contradicts the bruised feelings we're wrestling with inside as a result of our discouragements over ourselves, others, or reverses in our self-determined plans for our lives. Therefore, few people know us as we really are. That not only robs us of deep, caring relationships when we fall, but keeps us from experiencing intimacy with God. We become so accustomed to trying to have it all to-gether, that our conversation with Him in prayer takes on the same studied pretension. We pray about surface things with glib phrases and still continue to brood over our deepest concerns. Or what's worse, we take our blessings and achievements for granted, and our prayers lack the vibrancy of unfettered praise. We drift into bland prayers that neither plumb the sullen depths of anguish nor rise to the sublime heights of adoration. We endure our falls with self-incrimination or blame for others and claim our accomplishments as the due reward for our self-effort. We miss both the gracious arms of God drawing us into His greatness, and our own potential great-ness through Him.

The Psalms help us to learn how to pray honestly. Athanasius said, "Most Scripture speaks to us, while the Psalms speak for us." In each of the Psalms we enter into the experience of the psalmist as he pours out his heart to God. There is no human thought or emotion unexpressed in the Psalms. And each leads to a revelation of an aspect of the character of God. Our concerns and the character of God are brought together magnificently in the Psalms. It is remarkable how our concerns today were expressed by the psalmists so long ago. They praised the Lord in words we long to emulate in our own prayers. And yet they are no less authentic in the unbridled flow of their thoughts and feelings about the hurts, injustices, and problems of life. As we read the Psalms, we want to say, "That's exactly how I feel!" or "How could the psalmist know about what I've been through?" or "What the psalmist prayed is exactly what I most need to pray today!" We discover how to pray in the ups and downs of life.

The Psalms thus become the springboard of great prayer. Alex-ander Maclaren said, "If the rest of Scripture may be called the speech of the Spirit of God to man, this book [the Psalms] is the answer of the Spirit of God in man." The more we read and study the Psalms, the more our language takes on the dimension of depth. Our prayers become more real, authentic, and bold. And as a result, our inner self is invaded by the Lord Himself. We come to

Him as we are, and learn to know Him as He is. Our thoughts are remolded around the truth of His nature, and our emotions are liberated from self-imposed bondage.

When we pray through the Psalms we use the prayer book of the Lord Jesus Christ. We sense His presence as we underline verses that are prophetic of His life and death. We experience again the unfolding drama of the atonement and affirm the unity of the Scriptures as the Word of God.

We also become one with Christians through the ages. The early church used the Psalms as the first Christian hymnbook. The Reformation was spurred on by the reading and singing of the Psalms. Who can read Psalm 46 without joining his or her voice with Luther's in singing, "A mighty fortress is our God!"? In Scotland, the metrical paraphrases of the Psalms became the hymnbook of John Knox, and in years to follow, of Presbyterian churches throughout the world. All branches of the Christian church have utilized the Psalms in worship. Many of the great hymns in modern hymnbooks are based on the Psalms. Calvin said that the Psalms, "open up to us familiar access to God." Every age has turned to the Psalms for courage, comfort, and challenge.

The reason is that the psalmists accepted God's claim on their lives and responded with magnificent rhetoric which, though sometimes strange to our modern ear tuned to our contemporary idioms and metaphors, presses us into deeper communication with the Lord and, as a result, into greater creativity in our own prayers. Each time a psalm is read, prayed, sung, or studied, it gives us fresh insight into our needs and the God who can help us. John Donne said that the Psalms are, "like manna which tasted to every man like that he loved best." And I would add—what each person needs most. They speak to our condition. Our concerns are matched by our encounter with the many-splendored character of God.

Alexander Whyte, the famous Scottish preacher of another generation (1836–1921), once explained to his theological students, "Ah, I envy you young men with your ministry before you, and especially that you have ahead a lifetime of explaining the Psalms to your people!" I share Dr. Whyte's enthusiasm. But explaining the Psalms, or any portion of Scripture, must be done after listening to God and to people. When we listen intently to the expressed needs of people, the Psalms come alive in a new way as God's answer to those needs.

This book is in direct response to the concerns people have shared with me. Each chapter confronts the real life problems and perplexities we face today. Each is based on one or more of the Psalms. I try to identify the close similarity between what we are going through and what the psalmists prayed through. After establishing the common concern, I seek to get inside the psalmist's skin and feel and think with him as he grappled with life and came to a much more profound understanding of God's providence and power. The result is that our hearts become one with the authors of the Psalms. Each theme is illustrated with contemporary stories of people today. In conversation with you, the reader, I try to weave together biblical exposition, historical and contemporary scholarship, illustrations, and explanation that seeks to be both encouraging and empathetical.

My biggest problem when preparing this contemporary exposition of the Psalms was deciding which Psalms to select. Out of the treasure chest of one hundred and fifty psalms included in the Book of Psalms, which ones should I choose? Prolonged study over the years has made them all cherished favorites. However, there is a repetition of themes and ideas in many of them. Therefore, I wanted this book to represent the various types of psalms, a balanced proportion from each of the five sections of the Book of Psalms, and a treatment of the major themes. Most of all, my formula of choice was guided by those Psalms that spoke both for and to us in our needs today. The final test was based on the psalmist's ability to lead the reader to an encounter with an aspect of the character of God.

So whatever your need is right now as you begin reading this book, I think you'll find it addressed in the following pages. You may be experiencing one of life's many falls at this point in your life. We all have this in common: we have fallen at some time in life's race, or we may fall when we least expect it in the future, or we are urgently concerned about someone else who is falling and we long to help. What I have tried to share in this book is how to allow God to catch us when we fall and how to share that secret of falling into greatness with others.

I want to express my gratitude to Jerlyn Gonzalez, my administrative assistant, for typing my handwritten draft of the manuscript and then retyping through several revisions. Her faithfulness and patience is an expression of God's greatness, which she has experienced through His grace in her own life.

And to my wife, Mary Jane, I express special thanks for her partnership in living with me the thoughts shared in this book. We prayed through the Psalms together on vacation three years ago, and our thoughts shared together in those devotional times became the vision for this book. Nothing can happen *through* an author that has not happened *to* him. He can reproduce only what he is freshly rediscovering. I am thankful for Mary Jane's insights and comments on each chapter. Her greatness, profoundly deepened by her fall into God's arms during a time of sickness, was a living example for me in writing what follows.

LLOYD JOHN OGILVIE

1

The Secret of Lasting Joy
Psalm 1

The tone of the voice of an old friend on the phone alarmed me. What he said made his request that we get together over lunch to talk a top priority.

"I can't talk about it over the phone," he said urgently—grimly, "but I do need to see you. I've fallen into a terrible thing which I can't seem to shake. I desperately need to talk with someone."

I quickly rearranged my schedule for the next day and told him I'd meet him for lunch. When I hung up the phone, my mind raced to the possibilities of what might be hassling my friend.

What had happened to him? I wondered. My friend had been an energetic Christian who sought to follow Christ in his marriage, family life, and busy career in business. But I also knew that he had drifted away from the church and Christian fellowship in recent years. What had tripped him? What was causing the despondency I heard in his voice? Adultery? Some kind of shady business practice?

A Subtle Disease

When we sat down for lunch, we had barely begun the first course when he blurted out what was happening to him. "Lloyd, I've become a cynic! I've become a negative, critical, and sarcastic man."

I sighed with relief inside, grateful that he had not confessed some more heinous sin. But as I listened carefully to what he told

15

me, I realized that cynicism is no less a sin than if he had been sleeping with another woman or had embezzled the books of his business.

My friend had been jarred by the reality of the kind of person he had become because of an ultimatum his wife had given him. She was not willing to spend the rest of her life with a man who had come to be down on life, people, and even God. Several friends had confronted him about his snarling attitude. Three people had resigned from his company because they said they could not work in the negative atmosphere his attitudes had created. The man's world was falling apart.

The rest of the lunch time was spent talking about how my friend had gotten into the despondent mood that had manifested such cynicism. His surface analysis of what was causing his attitudinal problem was a sad tale of disappointments with people, business reversals, and exhaustion from the pressures at work. I pressed deeper to what I discerned were the real causes. I asked him about the people with whom he spent time and then about his relationship with the Lord. His answer exposed the problem. His confidants were as negative as he was, and he had drifted away from any consistent prayer or reading of the Bible. He felt that God had not answered his prayers, so what was the use of praying? If God knew or cared about him, he said, He either could not or would not do anything!

Do you know anyone like my friend? Ever feel the way he felt? Do you feel that way now? Cynicism is addictive. It begins with negativism, grows into a critical attitude, and becomes a settled personality trait. We all suffer from this debilitating, virulent poison to some degree. The opposite of joy is not glumness; it's cynicism. Robert Louis Stevenson said, "To lose the joy is to lose everything." And when the joy of our faith is lost, cynical attitudes take its place.

What do we do when we are tempted to become cynical because of life's frustrations, people who disappoint us, and when our capacity to hope seems depleted?

The first psalm gives us an analysis of and a prescription for the source of lasting joy as an antidote to grim cynicism. I used the passage that day as the biblical basis for counseling my friend. What I shared with him is what I want to talk over with you in this chapter. An exposition of Psalm 1 reveals joy as the gift of the blessed and cynicism as the besetting sin of the scoffer. The more I have studied this psalm, the more I have realized its application to the problem of negativism and despondency crippling so many Christians today.

Blessed is the Man!

The first psalm describes the true nature of blessedness. The Hebrew word for *blessed*, *'ashrê*, means happy or joyous. But a deeper penetration into the root meaning reveals the nature of that bliss. It comes from a verb meaning to go forth, to advance, or even to lead the way. All these nuances may be implied in what the psalmist depicted in the first verse of the psalm. His portrait of a joyous person is one who is pressing on in a life of clearly set goals and purpose. The blessed person is one who is energetically pressing ahead through life, grasping its many-splendored wonder. His eyes are on the Lord and His plan for him. Life is exciting; serendipities of grace await him each new day; expectation of unlimited possibilities makes his spirit vibrant with hope.

Surprisingly, the psalmist described what the blessed man does *not* do. He does not walk in the counsel of the ungodly, stand in the path of sinners, or sit in the seat of the scornful. From what we are told the blessed person has no time to do, we are given an apt description of how cynicism begins, grows, and becomes a settled attitudinal sin. The backsliding can happen to any of us when we slow down in what Paul called pressing "toward the goal for the prize of the upward call of God in Christ Jesus" (Phil. 3:14).

Three Steps to Cynicism

Cynicism begins when we take our eyes off the Lord and the goal of running with Him, paced by His purpose and plan. It begins

17

when we slow up and walk in the counsel of the ungodly. That means that we begin to listen to the advice of people who live their lives on their own strength and resources, who see life as it is without the Lord's presence and power.

Ungodly is not a descriptive word in our popular parlance anymore. The Hebrew word for ungodly, *rāsha'*, is also translated as "wicked," the compulsive determination to live life horizontally with no vertical dependence on supernatural power. This is the first step to cynicism.

Ungodly people are all around us. They influence our perception of life's possibilities. They are not always "bad" people, just "gray" people who assert by attitude and conviction, "If we can't do it, it can't be done." Because they depend solely on their own strength and their white-knuckled grip on life, they become easily discouraged and negative. Their attitudes are contagious. We are affected by their sour mood and grim outlook. Many of them write the analysis of the news in daily newspapers or drone their pessimism on television. Some are shaping our outlook by giving us the facts without faith in any hope beyond human skill and cleverness. The ungodly can live in our homes, work with us, be among our best friends. Taking their advice is fatal. The blessed person does not slow down to walk with them. If he does, his walk will soon come to an immobilizing standstill.

That's what the psalmist meant by standing in the path of sinners. The sinner's condition is worse than the ungodly. The ungodly live their lives without any dependence on God. The sinner excludes Him entirely. To sin means to miss the mark. Sinners have the wrong goals in life. They are heading in the wrong direction. Standing among them tempts us to miss our sublime purpose to "glorify God and enjoy Him forever."

Our use of the word *sinner* usually describes conduct. The Scriptures go deeper to expose the condition that causes that conduct. The Hebrew *haṭṭā'* denotes those who are living by the wrong values and goals. To stand in their path is eventually to go with them in a direction away from God. As walking with the ungodly influences our thinking, standing with sinners affects our behavior. Inadvertently, we become like the people with whom we associate. Cynicism starts with thought, it is expressed in attitude, and becomes a part of our being.

That happens when we sit down among the scornful. The Hebrew word is *lētsîm*, "scoffers," those who mock God. This kind of scoffing can be very subtle and veiled. At the heart of the scorn is pride. Pride puts itself above God, questions His ways, and lives life independent of a need for His guidance or power. You're probably saying, "That's the way most people live." You're right! And that's why it's difficult not to be infected by such an attitude. Cynicism is scoffing in its worst state.

As J. H. Jowett says in *Springs in the Desert*, "Whatsoever things are ugly, the cynic thinks on these things." The cynic's attention is focused on the inadequacy of the human race as a basis for keeping attention off his own failing. Every new calamity is further evidence of the dreary lot of life. He always looks for the fortification of his negative view of things in every human failure and every inexplicable disaster. If he believes in God at all, he thinks He is aloof from the problems and perplexities of daily living. The cynic is devoid of hope. When we sit among the scornful, the time isn't long before a permanent chair is reserved for us.

Sidestepping Cynicism

The psalmist says that the blessed person avoids the progressive steps to cynicism. Why? He doesn't need them. He has other resources. So in verses 2 and 3 we are given the antidote to cynicism. Verse 2 tells us what the cynic does to emerge from his condition, and verse 3 tells us what the Lord provides as an alternative to the cynic's negative view of things. In both verses, joy is implied.

19

Delighting in God's Word

The delight of the blessed person is the law of God. Artur Weiser in *The Psalms* speaks of the law as the "intelligible expression of the divine will, valid once and for all, and therefore as the unerring compass, which is able to regulate . . . conduct, but at the same time also as a strong bond of trust in God's providential rule over his life."[1] For the psalmist, the Law meant the Ten Commandments, but also the acts and words of God encompassed in the Pentateuch, the first five books of the Bible. For us as Christians, the implication is the whole Bible as a revelation of the ultimate will of God and the key to unlocking His specific guidance for particular directions and choices.

Our delight, the source of our joy, is to be the divinely inspired Word of God. Consistent, habitual daily reading provides us with an assurance of God's love, providence, and intervening grace. In His presence in Jesus Christ, we receive forgiveness, assurance of pardon, and affirmation of our worth as called, chosen, and cherished people. Added to the delight of God's Word is the privilege of meditating on its meaning for the challenges and complexities we face. Unlike the cynic, we have a positive perspective on life's perplexities. The only things that can ultimately hurt us are those we refuse to surrender to the Lord. When we commit our way to the Lord, He does one of two kinds of miracles: in some situations, He steps in to change things; in others, He gives us the courage to endure.

The word *meditation* is fascinating in its Hebrew etymology. It not only meant to think about the Lord's Word in the Torah, but also to read it aloud with a low, chanting tone. Reading the Scriptures aloud gave the Hebrew person focused attention and learning by eye and ear. The same word is used in Scripture for a young lion growling over its prey, for the murmuring of a dove, and as a synonym for "to remember and muse on." It is frequently used for a cow chewing its cud, a creature who masticates its food thoroughly.

What is implied by the psalmist is that our meditation is to make the law our nature and character. We are to be immersed, soaked thoroughly, inundated with the truth of God's Word.

Reading the Bible and prayer becomes a two-part alternative to cynicism. We learn His ways. Our minds become vibrant with what He has said in similar situations to those we face today. Also, our responses to life become controlled in what great saints have said in response to the complexities of life. When we pray, we claim the promises God has given us in Scripture.

Memorization of Scripture makes the Word a part of us. With it ingrained in our being, we can follow Paul's admonition to "Pray without ceasing" (1 Thess. 5:17). And in our prayers we can carry on a conversation about the implications of God's will for us. We become fortified against discouragement and negativism.

I know such a practice works. Some years ago, I made a commitment to memorize each week the passage I selected to preach on and the correlating Scriptures used in the body of the sermon. The result is I have a vast reservoir of refortifying truth for any situation.

Like you, I am tempted to become discouraged at times. People disappoint me, and I become impatient with groups and institutions. But I know when I am becoming disillusioned, and I realize that it's time to pray, to put my eyes back on the Lord and not on my judgments of people or their reactions.

Meditation on the Law is only the first step of what the psalmist claimed for the blessing. Prayer and meditation on the Scriptures opens us to the indefatigable resources of the Spirit of the Lord.

God's Alternative

The blessed are "like a tree planted by the rivers of water" (v. 3). What is implied is that they are transplanted and rooted by the river. The simile is of a palm tree, which is able to draw from the unlimited flow of the river beside which it is growing. As a result, it is stable. Firmly rooted, the tree stands erect, in spite of wind and changing weather. It has strength because of its roots' reaching to the river's resources. It is secure and stately, and its substance is produced in fruit in its season. We are meant to live like that.

In Scripture, the river is a magnificent metaphor of the Spirit of the Lord. The term *rivers of water* is used often for His presence and power. In Psalm 46:4, the psalmist wrote,

> There is a river whose streams shall
>   make glad the city of God.
> The holy place of the tabernacle of the
>   Most High.
> God is in the midst of her,
>   she shall not be moved;
> God shall help her,
>   just at the break of dawn.

The Lord used the same metaphor for His presence in Ezekiel's vision of the healing water and trees.

> Then he brought me back to the door of the temple; and there was water, flowing from under the threshold of the temple toward the east, for the front of the temple faced east; the water was flowing from under the right side of the temple, south of the altar. He brought me out by way of the north gate, and led me around on the outside to the outer gateway that faces east; and there was water, running out on the right side. . . . Then he said to me: "This water flows toward the eastern region, goes down into the valley, and enters the sea. When it reaches the sea, its waters are healed. And it shall be that every living thing that moves, wherever the rivers go, will live. There will be a very great multitude of fish, because these waters go there; for they will be healed, and everything will live wherever the river goes" (Ezek. 47:1–2, 8–9).

Jesus offered the Samaritan woman water that would quench her deepest thirst. He said, "'Whoever drinks of the water that I shall give him will never thirst. But the water that I shall give him will become in him a fountain of water springing up into everlasting life'" (John 4:14). Later, during the Feast of Tabernacles, He observed the ritual of a priest's carrying a golden pitcher containing three logs (about two pints) of water from the Pool of Siloam to the temple and pouring it on the altar. He stepped forward and made this bold claim: ". . . 'If anyone thirst, let him come to Me and drink. He who believes in Me, as the Scripture has said, out of his heart will flow rivers of living water'" (John 7:37–38).

John's comment on this bold promise was made in the context of the return of the resurrected, glorified Christ in the power of the Holy Spirit. "But this He spoke concerning the Spirit, whom those believing in Him would receive; for the Holy Spirit was not yet given, because Jesus was not yet glorified" (John 7:39).

After the ascension and glorification of Christ, the Holy Spirit came at Pentecost and filled Christ's disciples with His power. Paul reflects on this in Galatians—". . God has sent forth the Spirit of His Son into your hearts . . ." (4:6)—and in Colossians— ". . . Christ in you, the hope of glory" (Col. 1:27). The river of life for us is the living Christ who is present with us and in us. His promise, coupled with the psalmist's image, makes a powerful picture. His Spirit is like a river flowing through us—in our minds, emotions, wills, and bodies.

Following the imagery of the psalmist in this first psalm, we bring forth our fruit, our leaf does not wither, and whatever we do prospers. Let's consider that more fully. The fruit of the Water of Life in us is Christ's mind, character, and disposition. Paul admonished the Philippians, "Let this mind be in you which was also in Christ Jesus" (2:5).

The word for *mind* used here also means disposition. When we are rooted in Christ, we think His thoughts and respond to life with His disposition. Further, the fruit of Christ's indwelling, artesian waters, is the development of His character traits in us. Galatians 5:22–23 describes what we are to become: "The fruit of the Spirit is

23

love, joy, peace, longsuffering, kindness, goodness, faithfulness, gentleness, self-control. . . ."

What could better describe the *opposite* of cynicism? Christ's flowing in us produces His own response to the problems of life. Instead of walking in the counsel of the ungodly, we can walk in fellowship with Christ. "As you have therefore received Christ Jesus the Lord, so walk in Him, rooted and built up in Him and established in the faith . . ." (Col. 2:6–7). The violent winds of life will not uproot us.

What Paul prayed for the Ephesians is our promise, too! "That Christ may dwell in your hearts through faith; that you, being rooted and grounded in love, may be able to comprehend with all the saints what is the width and length and depth and height—to know the love of Christ which passes knowledge; that you may be filled with all the fullness of God" (Eph. 3:17–19).

As we meditate on that love, chew on it, think it through, and sing it forth, we are filled with new joy. We are not alone. The roots of our hearts and minds are planted deeply in Christ. The width, length, depth, and height of His river of love give us confidence to replace any cynicism that may have begun to grow in our thinking and attitude. We are blessed indeed!

A Contrast in Destiny

To heighten our gratitude for being blessed, the psalmist describes the destiny of those who do not have roots in the river. The ungodly, those who live without the strength available to them, are described in three vivid ways.

First, they are "like the chaff which the wind drives away" (v. 4). What a striking contrast to a well-rooted tree! A review of the threshing methods of biblical times is helpful here. The sheaves of harvested grain were laid out on the threshing floor and a wooden sled was drawn back and forth over them, crushing the stalks and breaking open the ears of grain.

The grain then needed to be separated from the empty husks and crushed stalks or straw. This was done by tossing the lot into the air. The wind would catch the chaff (the empty husks and straw) and blow it away. The grain would fall to the ground and be gathered into bins, later to be ground into flour.

The chaff became a picturesque way of referring to those who did not know or trust God. Like the chaff, they were worthless, without fruit or value. As chaff was impermanent and unstable, so those who knew not God were light and easily blown by the shifting ways of opinion or adversity. That leads to the second warning.

Carrying the metaphor further, the psalmist pointed out that those without God are to be separated. He warned that the ungodly cynic cannot survive the judgment. That's what the psalmist meant when he said, "Therefore the ungodly shall not stand in the judgment . . ." (v. 5). What is the judgment? We must interpret it in the light of Jesus Christ. This judgment is in effect daily on our thoughts and actions, but it is also a final judgment. If we choose to live without the Lord in this life, we will live apart from Him and the bliss of heaven for eternity. Simply put, we get what we want.

The cynic would be very uncomfortable in heaven! Who would listen to his complaints, his cutting criticism of the Lord, and his deriding negativism? Hell (whatever our picture of eternal separation from God) will certainly be a maze of collected cynicism around the chief cynic, the Devil.

The third warning of the psalmist is that the ungodly will not be part of the congregation of the righteous. When the Lord calls His people together, the ungodly cynic will not be there. This congregation of the righteous is not only an eternal privilege, but also fellowship with the Lord's people now. The cynic, by his own choice, denies the warmth and acceptance of fellowship. Who can measure up to his seething criticisms? Who is worthy of being trusted?

The cynic eventually has few, if any, friends. He is a loner in whom no one dares to confide. Who knows who will be the next candidate for his sarcastic, satirical suspicion and carping comments? The psalmist has forced us to see not only the danger of walking, standing, or sitting among the company of the cynics, but he also has shown us their fate.

The psalm comes to a close with an even more shocking comparison. "The LORD knows the way of the righteous, but the way of the ungodly shall perish" (v. 6). The word *know* in Hebrew is a cornucopia filled with meaning. It means intimate ownership, relationship, and companionship. Here in Psalm 1, to *know* implies more than aloof acknowledgment of the righteous. Even more than aquaintanceship, it is abiding fellowship.

And who are the righteous? The psalmist talks of those who are the blessed, but in the light of the life, message, and atoning death of Jesus Christ, the righteous are those who have been made right with God through the substitutionary sacrifice of the cross. Christ is the righteousness of God, and through Him and in Him we become righteous.

Christ assumed our sin and went to the cross to suffer for us. "For He made Him who knew no sin to be sin for us, that we might become the righteousness of God . . ." (2 Cor. 5:21). We are given the gift of faith to accept that righteousness through the cross. So we affirm with Paul, "I am not ashamed of the gospel of Christ, for it is the power of God to salvation for everyone who believes, for the Jew first and also for the Greek, for in it the righteousness of God is revealed from faith to faith; as it is written 'The just shall live by faith'" (Rom. 1:16–17). By faith alone we are accepted as the righteous men and women of God. That faith is the missing ingredient of the ungodly cynic. His way will perish.

Hope for the Cynic

What hope, then, is there for the cynic? His deepest need is for rebirth, to begin all over again. That, too, presses us on to the gospel, for the Lord had a special concern for cynics. (Thomas is the patron saint of cynics who are transformed by the power of the Lord's undeniable love.)

At the core of the cynic's heart is the desperate need for love. He is the negative, critical person he is because he cannot believe in himself or anyone else. And so our study of Psalm 1 takes on a strange twist. How shall we love the cynic in Christ's name and by His power without walking, standing, or sitting with him? Once we see the danger of cynicism, we can allow the Lord to extricate us from its grasp. Then we can have a ministry to cynics without being sucked into the whirlpool of their negative thinking. If we draw deeply from the river of living water, we no longer need to be cynical and can care for those who are. No longer intimidated by them, we can share the reason for the hope within us.

That's essentially what I tried to do that day over lunch with my friend who had become cynical. He desperately needed a rebirth experience, a fresh beginning. He needed to know that he was loved and that the Lord was in charge of his future. He knew that further cynicism would destroy his life—marriage, friends, and business.

"Do you want to change?" I asked him. He said he did. We left the restaurant and sat in his car. In a brief time of prayer, he let go of his arrogant judgmentalism and allowed the Lord's love to flood his empty soul. The river of living water replaced the parched cynicism. He left his seat among the scornful and turned his life over to the Lord.

I have seen him often since that day, and he is discovering the daily power that comes from the river of life, Christ Himself. The psalmist would call him a blessed man. He has the secret of lasting joy.

2

Living at Full Potential
Psalm 8

I want you to join me in a grand experiment. For just a moment imagine you have God's vision and heart. Now I want you to see yourself from His perspective and vision for your life. Looking at yourself, your life, and the realm of your responsibility, what do you see?

A Twin Barometer

Two things will determine what you see: (1) your conception of God, and (2) your own attitude toward your life. If your idea of God is limited to one of a cosmic judge who is full of wrath for your failures and mistakes, what you will see of yourself through His eyes will be confining and oppressive. If, however, your image of God is that He forgives even before you ask, He loves you unreservedly, and He wants the very best for your life, you will see yourself through His eyes of hope for your future.

Chances are your own attitude toward yourself is projected onto God. If you are down on yourself and expect little for your future, that will probably be what you think God sees when He looks at your life. Even if you have a healthy self-appreciation, it is most likely that your view of your potential is only one percent of what He sees is possible for your life.

Getting outside ourselves and seeing our potential from God's perspective is a liberating and exciting experience. Contemplation of the majesty of God results in an awesome experience of the magnificence of His vision of our potential.

That's what happened to King David when he prayed what he wrote down in the eighth psalm. He began his prayers with a salutation which literally set his mind reeling about God and about the entrusted authority and power He has given to humankind. The words, "O LORD our Lord" (v. 1) combine two Hebrew names for God that describe His creative and sustaining nature and His personal involvement in running the universe: *Yahweh our Adonai*.

Yahweh comes from the Hebrew letters YHWH, which probably derive from the basic verb *hāyah*, "to be." That is how God first identified Himself to Moses at the burning bush, "I am that I am" or "I will be whom I will be." God is the uncreated creator, unmoved mover, the one who made the universe out of nothing and in whom all the galaxies maintain their place and purpose. That creator and sustainer of the universe is also our *Adonai*; the absolute ruler, king, and sovereign of all life.

The personal pronoun *our* knits the two names together in sublime meaning for us. He is our Lord because He has elected us to be His people. We are chosen before we choose to call Him our Lord. He made us for a relationship with Him. We know who He is and what He is like only because He has graciously chosen to reveal Himself. When we dare to see ourselves in His eyes, we must begin where the psalmist began—with the realization that our Lord is the source and sustainer of our existence. What He sees is the only ultimately reliable and important evaluation. He is the One on whom our life is totally dependent and to whom we are responsible.

The Names of God

That led the psalmist to begin to think about the names of his God. "How excellent is Your name in all the earth,/You who set Your glory above the heavens!" (v. 1). The name *excellent* means excelling all others. God's name—His character—is that which is

majestic, mighty, and glorious. The psalmist's meaning is exposed
by Psalm 20:7, "Some trust in chariots, and some in horses;/But we
will remember the name of the LORD our God." Remembering His
name was to contemplate God's revealed nature. The key word here
is "glory." *Kābôd* in Hebrew comes from a verb meaning value,
weight, or wealth. God owns the universe and as its creator is po-
tentate of the heavens and the earth.

The psalmist's heart swelled with praise. The Lord's praise is sung
in the highest heaven, but also out of the mouths of babes and
infants. Dahood, in the *Anchor Bible: Psalms I*, translates "Out of
the mouth of babes and infants/You have ordained strength" (v. 2)
as, "I will adore Your majesty above the heavens,/With the lips of
striplings and sucklings."[1] God is praised by angels and by the
childlike adoration of the psalmist.

Jesus quoted this verse when the leaders of Israel tried to silence
the crowd's unbridled praise for Him during the triumphal entry
into Jerusalem. This is a clear indication of His claim to being the
divine Messiah, but it is also an acknowledgment of the inherent
yearning in us to praise. Praise cannot be silenced by the enemy or
the avenger. Jesus said that if the leaders of Israel tried to silence the
crowd, even the stones would cry out adoration for the Lord.

The Creation

The psalmist continued his praise as he contemplated the heavens above which God's glory is set.

> When I consider Your heavens,
>   the work of Your fingers,
> The moon and the stars,
>   which You have ordained,
> What is man that You are mindful of him,
> And the son of man that You visit him?" (vv. 3–4).

The immensity of the heavens held the psalmist in a spell of wonderment. With his naked eye on a clear night, he could see about five thousand stars. Today with a four-inch telescope we can see more than two million, and with the Mount Palomar two-hundred-inch mirror, we are able to see more than a billion. The latest means of observation reveal even greater numbers. The expanse is beyond our comprehension. If we set out and traveled at space rocket speed of 19,000 miles per hour, it would take 144,000 years to reach the nearest star. We measure the universe in light years rather than miles. The speed of light is 186,000 miles per second, so that in a year of seconds, light travels six trillion miles. This distance is called a light year. Calculation shows that it is equal to 60,000 times the distance of the sun from the earth. The universe is so vast that to cross it at the speed of light, you would travel forty billion light years.

Mere Man

No wonder, even with his limited knowledge, the psalmist asked the question, "What is man that You are mindful of him,/And the son of man that You visit him?" *Son of man* in this usage means mere man. The psalmist expressed his astonishment that God even knows about the planet Earth, let alone cares about the creature man who lives upon it. But Yahweh not only knows, He cares and comes to His people with love and compassion.

But that's not all! God has made man "a little lower than the angels . . ." (v. 5). The word for *angels* in Hebrew is *'ĕlōhîm*, a name of God. It also has been translated as angelic beings or judges. The meaning for us is exhilarating at whatever level it is interpreted. I choose "a little lower than God" because of what follows: ". . . And You have crowned him with glory and honor" (v. 5). These are attributes of God Himself.

Glory, as we have noted, means value and magnitude of potential. Ability and power would also be implied. *Honor* is recognition of status and strength. That idea is amplified by the next verse, "You have made him to have dominion over the works of Your hands;/ You have put all things under his feet." Our entrusted dominion over the created world is an expression of the glory and honor God has given us.

The psalmist enumerated the extent of this dominion by blurting out in wonderment, "All sheep and oxen—/Even the beasts of the field,/The birds of the air,/And the fish of the sea . . ." Everything in the created order of the earth is under our command. We are nearer to God than the heavens, and the earth was created for us! How can we respond? Worship. Only praise and adoration suffice. And then we come full circle with the psalmist and repeat the words with which he began. "O LORD, our Lord,/How excellent is Your name in all the earth!" (v. 9).

As we linger in adoration, something else happens within us. We are struck with the realization of our responsibility. If God has given us dominion, then we are responsible to Him for how we exercise our calling. We teeter on the sharp edge of pride and authentic humility. The exaltation of man in Psalm 8 must be coupled with the constant reminder of the theme of Psalm 24:1: "The earth is the LORD's, and all its fullness,/The world and those who dwell therein." We do not own the world; we are only given dominion. The Lord is King, and He has called us to be viceroys of His delegated management. We have no authority or power apart from a dependent relationship with Him.

There's the rub! Humankind denied that dependency on God and wanted to claim ultimate authority over life and the world. We "exchanged the truth of God for the lie, and worshiped and served the creature rather than the Creator, who is blessed forever." (Rom. 1:25). The psalmist did not include the fall of man in his hymn of praise, yet, perhaps it was on his mind. We wonder if his exuberant praise was not mingled with sorrow over the realization of what humankind was destined to be and had become. Psalms 9 and 10 deal with man's evil and rebellion. The enemies of God are those who have arrogantly misused His entrusted dominion. When we rise to the heights of Psalm 8 and fall to the depths of realizing what we have done with our "glory and honor," we know why Jesus Christ had to come.

A fascinating note to this study is the fact that the author of Hebrews quoted the eighth psalm as a messianic psalm that foretells the life of the Savior. As the early church looked back it saw Jesus, the new Adam, as One worthy of the marvelous accolade of the psalm. He truly was crowned with glory and honor and put all things under His feet—even death. Paul also sounded this note in the Corinthian letter.

> For He must reign till He has put all enemies under His feet. The last enemy that will be destroyed is death. For 'He has put all things under His feet.' But when He says 'all things are put under Him,' it is evident that He who put all things under Him is excepted. Now when all things are made subject to Him, then the Son Himself will also be subject to Him who put all things under Him, that God may be all in all (1 Cor. 15:25–28).

The apostle's words give us the sense of the resurrected Lord's continuing ministry until the end of history. Christ continues to subject the enemies of life, and He works through us to help us claim the sublime stature we were created to know and experience. It is only as Christ makes us new creatures that we are able to accept humbly the grandeur of the psalmist's words. The Lord sees us through the dilated focus of Calvary and the Resurrection and the Pentecost effluence of His Spirit. As we accept His death for our sins, are resurrected to newness of life, and are regenerated by His indwelling Spirit, then we are able to exercise the dominion entrusted to us. Awe, joy, humility, and then responsibility flow as a natural result.

Especially for Us

Psalm 8 must be considered within the context of Jesus' teaching on the kingdom of God. The keynote of His message, the witness of

His life, and the purpose of H s death were to make the promise of the psalm a reality. The kingdom of God is His realm, reign, and rule in us, between us in our relationships, and through us in all the affairs of life. We enter the kingdom by rebirth, we grow in it by a constant reliance on the King, and we realize its full impact as we seek and do the King's will. Delegated authority, plus dependence on the One who gives the authority, equals dominion.

In the light of all this, we are ready to grapple with the personal implications of this psalm for us today. Each of us has been entrusted with a realm of responsibility. Our sphere of dominion begins with ourselves, encompasses our relationships, and spreads to the structures of society where we work, live, and are governed. The Lord has given us glory and honor as His agents to be stewards of life. He made the earth and its resources for us. He endowed us with intellect, emotion, will, and body to enjoy the delights of living. We are responsible to Him for what we do with the potential He has given us.

Psalm 8 is a clarion call to live at full potential in the sphere of the kingdom of God entrusted to us. What was said of Esther can be said of each of us. "You have come to the kingdom for such a time as this" (Esth. 4:14). Such a time and such a place no one else can fill.

That leads us to the steps necessary for living out the glory and honor the Lord has bestowed on us.

1. *Claim your realm*. Whoever we are, we have a realm given to us by the Lord. That is our sphere, our assignment, and we cannot sidestep it. The joy of life is in its responsibilities. They are not a drudgery, but the essence of creative living. Think of your realm as the combination of the relationships and responsibilities of life. Knowing that you are crowned with the Lord's glory and honor, picture what you would do and be if you lived at maximum for Him in your realm. What would you be as a person if excellence were the irreducible maximum? If we have the power of self-limitation, we also are capable of being greater than we are. That presses us to the second step.

2. *Consecrate your realm*. All that we have and are is a gift of the Lord. He entrusts our realm to us so that we consecrate it to Him. That means surrendering all our affairs to His guidance and direction. Our purpose is to discover and do His will in our realm.

Daily prayer at the beginning and end of each day and moment by moment prayers throughout the day enable us to relinquish our realm of responsibility and relationships to Him. He has not called us to work independently from Him in our realm, but dependently, to allow Him to work through us. The wonder of our creation is that we can think the thoughts of God, will to do what His wisdom clarifies, and live to His glory.

Consecration of our realm begins with ourselves. Have we ever surrendered all that we are to the Lord? Have we allowed Him to give us power to live at full potential? Next, consider our families and friends. Are we helping them realize their potential? That requires involvement, caring, affirmation, and gracious accountability. We all should be able to expect that people would say of us,

> Not merely in the words you say,
>   Not in your deeds confessed,
> But in the most unconscious way
>   Is Christ expressed.
> Is it a beatific smile?
>   A holy light upon your brow?
> Oh no! I felt His presence while
>   You laughed just now.
> For me 'twas not the truth you taught
>   To you so clear, to me so dim,
> But when you came to me you brought
>   A sense of Him.
> And from your eyes He beckons me,
>   And from your heart His love is shed
> Till I lose sight of you—and see
>   The Christ instead.[2]

When that happens we will be able not only to teach but also to share how people can discover both abundant and eternal life in Christ. Give the Lord the people of your life and ask Him to reveal His glory and honor so vividly through you that people will want a "reason for the hope that is in you" (1 Pet. 3:15). Has anyone asked you lately? Why not? We are to be reproducers of our faith in the relationships of our realm.

But consecrating our realm also means a social responsibility. We have been called to be intercessors for all of life, which includes our church, our community, and our nation. That call will mean action to implement our prayers. Every vital Christian I know is involved not only in sharing his or her faith with individuals, he or she also has asked the Lord to put on his or her agenda the special area of human suffering or need He has ordained as the focus of a ministry of reconciliation. The consecration of our realm requires the third step of exercising our dominion.

3. *Commit yourself to excellence in your realm.* The impact of the promise of Psalm 8 is that the Lord enables His excellence in us. How does this happen? When the living Christ takes up residence in us, He changes us into His likeness. Our goals become His goals, our standards His standards. We are given supernatural power for our responsibilities and relationships. A commitment to excellence in everything cannot be accomplished by us. We are weak and often accept second or even third best.

In order to encourage and motivate us, the Lord helps us to live in day-tight compartments. He forgives the past and guides the future. We can live today as if it were the only day we had. In the opportunity of the day we are called to dare to imagine what excellence might be by His power in us. Then we can pull out all the stops and let Him work through us. Emerson was right,

> Could'st thou in vision see
> Thyself, the man God meant;
> Thou never more wouldst be,
> The man thou art—content.

But we can see the vision. The Lord gives us the imagination to see any day lived in excellence for Him. Then He takes the responsibility of pulling it off through us. Through Christ, we are indeed, a little lower than *'ĕlōhîm*.

Luther claimed we were meant to be "a race of Christs." Awesome? Yes! But Christ does it. Paul had discovered this centuries earlier. He called the Philippians to enjoy his secret. ". . . whatever things are true, whatever things are noble, whatever things are just, whatever things are pure, whatever things are lovely, whatever things are of good report, if there is any virtue and if there is anything praiseworthy—meditate on these things" (Phil. 4:8). Christ Himself exhibits all these characteristics. When they are the focus of our picture of what can happen in any one day, He will work in us to make it possible. This results in a humble reverence and joyful praise in which both arrogance or discouragement are avoided.

 We have dared to feel with the Lord's heart and to see with His eyes. What we have felt and seen is the person we can be at full potential. The only time to begin to live that is today and the only place to claim it is right where we are. Then we can pray:

> Lord of all being, throned afar
> Thy glory flames from sun to star;
> Center and soul of every sphere,
> Yet to each loving heart how near![3]

3

The Apple of God's Eye
Psalm 17

Are you ever hurt by what people say to you or about you to others? Are you ever distressed when you are misunderstood, misinterpreted, or misused? Do you ever ache inside when the opinions of others go against you?

What about the times you can't explain yourself and gain affirmation of your values or actions? Do you ever feel defensive when you are attacked? Can people throw you into a tailspin when they maliciously criticize or destructively gossip about you?

Most of us would have to respond with a painful yes! We've all had times when we've been maligned by others.

Handling the Hurts

Those times can happen in a marriage, among people who work with us, for whom we work, or those who work for us. People can be cruel in what they say, even people who are supposed to be our friends. Sometimes those who hurt us are people in opposing political parties or people who hold different convictions from ours. Then there are those who question our theology and even cast suspicions on our relationship with God.

What do you do when someone becomes a self-appointed reformer with the focused purpose of straightening you out? It hurts, doesn't it? Our inner emotions reverberate for days after encounters with people like that. Sometimes the hurt lasts for months. When our integrity is challenged, the memory of the cutting criticism lingers for years. Perhaps you're feeling like that right now. You don't want to become an unfeeling person, but often repeated hurts build layers of scar tissue. We don't want to be hurt anymore, so we say we don't care what people think. But we do! We become imprisoned in the bondage of our hurt feelings.

What can we do? How can we be open to learn from what people say without getting caught in the whirling, downward spiraling of the cyclone of discouragement? Is there a creative way of sorting out the truth in what people may say? How do we separate their confused motives from what we may need to hear? They may have committed the treason of saying the right thing for the wrong reason or the wrong thing for the right reason. Some people can be written off with a "consider the source" self-justification. Others are significant, admired people in our lives, and we cannot easily dismiss what they say. The hurt is no less severe, however, when our personalities or characters are challenged.

How we wish we had more of a sense of humor when we are maligned by unthinking people! There's a wonderful story of a man who received a letter. On the stationery only one word was printed in bold, black letters: "Stupid!" The man's immediate response was to say, "I receive many letters which the sender forgot to sign. This is the first one that was signed and the writer forgot to write the message!"

But what about letters of demeaning criticism that are signed? We are forced to evaluate what's written and who signed them. Lots of energy can be expended reacting to what people write or say, and often hurts from our past intensify what's said to or about us. We overreact because of unresolved memories. Dealing with the matter is difficult whether the present or the past hurt inflames us. We become so defensive that we may explode with indignation and miss something we may need to hear. People say, "Why are you so upset? I just made a suggestion and you act as if I've declared war on you!"

What about *our* negative criticism of people? The amazing thing about us as people is that even though we know how much debilitating words hurt us, often we hurt others. In fact, people who have been hurt are often the most destructive in their words. Strange, isn't it? You'd think that our own smarting emotions would make us determined never to hurt anyone as we've been hurt. Not so. We repeat the cycle.

Alexander Whyte, the great Scottish preacher of another generation, asked three questions when tempted to level cutting criticism: Is it true? Is it necessary? Is it helpful? The same questions can be asked when we are hurt by what people say. Often all three questions can be answered yes, and we can learn and grow through what's said to us.

But such an attitude is dependent on a daily communion with the Lord in prayer, in which we gain perspective and stability. He wants to help us sort out what He may be saying to us through other people, regardless of their personal natures, which may be combative or competitive. The Lord desires to make us so secure in His love that we are able to allow Him to give us the courage to change if the criticism is true and the fortitude to endure when it is false.

The Setting of the Psalm

David was under fire when he wrote the seventeenth psalm. Many biblical expositors suggest this psalm was written when he was forced to flee because of Saul's neurotic jealousy of him.

You remember the story. David's slaying of Goliath gained him recognition and adulation. He became one of Saul's most gallant warriors. When he rose to power as a leader of Saul's armies and distinguished himself in battle, the people foolishly compared him to the king. They chanted, "Saul has slain his thousands, and David his ten thousands!" (1 Sam. 18:7).

The king grew suspicious and then was gripped with panic over

David's popularity. Though the young warrior remained faithful to Saul, the king's jealousy made him an enemy. A price was placed on his head and he had to flee for safety.

Probably during one of the long nights in flight, his exiled heart turned to the Lord for strength and courage in the midst of hostile accusations and charges of treason against the king and blasphemy against God. The psalm David prayed becomes a source of guidance for us on how and what to pray when we ache inside over false criticism and unfair judgments.

When we need the Lord's perspective and power in conflict, the psalm helps us regain an assurance of His love and a desire to open our hurting hearts to His healing. When we answer yes to the question of the old gospel hymn, "Do thy friends despise, forsake thee?" David's words show us how to "take it to the Lord in prayer."

Before we make any response to what people say to or about us, we need to look God in the eye. That's what David did. And what he saw in the eyes of God is the thrust of what I want to share in this chapter.

The Buck Stops There

The psalm begins where we must start. David presents his case to the highest court of appeal.

> Hear a just cause, O LORD.
> Attend to my cry;
> Give ear to my prayer that is not from deceitful lips.
> Let my vindication come from Your presence;
> Let *Your eyes look* on the things that are upright
>   (vv. 1–2; italics added).

The first thing we do when we are hurt by people, before we make any response, is to spread the whole matter out before the Lord. Allow His eyes to look at all the issues, the mixed motives, and the deeper reasons behind what has hurt us. We can ask,

"Lord, is there anything You are seeking to teach me in what has been said about me? Is there any truth in it? Your evaluation and judgment is all that is ultimately important."

David did that. He examined himself under the penetrating eyes of the Lord and exonerated himself of the charge of treason. Then he sought His vindication. He did not try to justify himself, but asked for the Lord's affirmation.

Inside of all of us is a dynamic center where the Lord looks. We know what we've done and been. We do not need to hide from the Lord or ourselves. In His presence, we do not need to defend ourselves or wilt under the pressure of other people's opinions. That kind of honesty with God enables us to say with Cromwell, "I know that God is above all reports; and that He will in His own time vindicate me." But even if that retribution doesn't happen in a way that satisfies our sense of justice, the Lord's vindication is all we need. We know that He does not wink at our sins when He looks at us. When people's words about us lead us to God for His judgment, we can be sure He will help us change whatever needs to be changed and refortify us when people's opinions are wrong.

So many of us live with unresolved guilt over past failures. When we are criticized, the new accusation touches the raw nerve that is attached to that old, unhealed memory. Unresolved guilt makes us vulnerable to respond with self-incrimination even when we are not guilty. Too quickly we buckle under, saying, "You're probably right. I'm wrong, wrong, wrong!" even when we may not be.

A Lesson from the Tax Man

A friend of mine was called by his tax consultant and told that the IRS had questioned his income tax return and had made an additional charge. Without investigating the reason he said, "Pay it! Pay it." He assumed he was wrong, when all the IRS wanted was an explanation.

But the tax consultant was a wise man and a good friend. He said quietly, "Sounds like some old fears have reared their ugly head. Don't assume you've made a mistake until we are sure you have!"

The same thing could be said about so much of our reaction to criticism. The Lord helps to deal with past failures so we can be honest with ourselves in the present. What a comfort! We can own our true guilt and be forgiven, and we can disown false guilt and live with assurance.

The source of lasting integrity is in God alone. David experienced the comfort of that. He went inward to the living center of his soul to investigate the possibility of wrong. He found no just reason for the accusations. He was not defensive but honestly analytical. Self-vindication was not enough; he had to experience the exoneration of the Lord. We need that exoneration, too, when general guilt feelings become so pervasive that we feel guilty every time we are criticized. The Lord wants to set us free from that syndrome. Only His grace can release us from that kind of soul malady.

David presented his case before the Lord and felt His lovingkindness. He continued his prayer in quest for that above all else. "You have tested my heart;/You have visited me in the night;/You have tried me and found nothing . . ." (v. 3). Having felt the painful slashes of people's cutting accusations, David committed himself not to return evil for evil.

> . . . I have purposed that my mouth shall not transgress.
> Concerning the works of men,
> By the word of Your lips,
> I have kept myself from the paths of the destroyer.
> Uphold my steps in Your paths,
> That my footsteps may not slip (vv. 3–5).

The Apple of His Eye

David opened himself to the eye of the Lord. He wanted the Lord to see him as he really was. Then he was prepared to look God in the eye. He prayed, "Keep me as the apple of Your eye;/Hide me under the shadow of Your wings" (v. 8).

The idiom *apple of Your eye*, by the way, is used repeatedly in Scripture. The Hebrew actually means "the little man of your eye" or "the daughter of the eye," based on what we see when we look a person in the eye at a very close range. We see the image of ourselves. If we stand close to a person we see the reflection of ourselves. Apply that to an intimate relationship with God and it means that He is looking at us, we are the focus of His attention, and that we can see ourselves as we are only when we see ourselves in His eyes.

Another interpretation of *apple of Your eye* is that God cherishes and values us as we do our own eyesight. The apple of the eye could mean the pupil of the eye.

Charles Spurgeon takes this tack in expositing the verse:

No part of the body is more precious, more tender and more carefully guarded than the eye; and of the eye, no portion more peculiarly to be protected than the central apple, the pupil, or as the "daughter of the eye." The all wise Creator has placed the eye in a well protected position; it stands surrounded by projecting bones like Jerusalem encircled by mountains. Moreover, its great Author has surrounded it with many tunics of inward covering, besides the hedge of the eyebrows, the curtain of the eyelashes, and the fence of the eyelids; and in addition to this, he has given to every man so high a value to his eyes, and so quick an apprehension of danger, that no member of the body is more faithfully cared for than the organ of sight.[1]

Thus, as we value the pupils of our eyes and the wonder of sight, so, too, the Lord cherishes each of us.

The most significant implication of this for our discussion of dealing with the hurts of life is that the delight of the Lord over us is the antidote for the discouragement caused by people's words. He sees us, knows and cares, and will not forsake us. That unqualified love heals our hurts. We feel unlimited grace when we feel that we are the apple of God's eye. We see ourselves reflected in His eye not as the person we've been, but as the miracle we can become.

Near the end of his life, Moses looked back and called the Israelites to praise the Lord for His constant care.

> For the LORD's portion is His people;
> Jacob is the place of His inheritance.
> He found him in a desert land
> And in the wasteland, a howling wilderness;
> He encircled him, He instructed him,
> He kept him as the apple of His eye (Deut. 32:9–10).

Surely that's what David had on his mind when he claimed again the Lord's choosing and calling of him to be His anointed. He could take anything as long as he knew he was being kept by the Lord. The ancient benediction became real to him.

> The LORD bless you and keep you;
> The LORD make His face shine upon you,
> And be gracious to you;
> The LORD lift up His countenance upon you,
> And give you peace (Num. 6:24–26).

And that's exactly what happened as David felt the Lord's acceptance and affirmation of him as the apple of His eye.

Have you ever heard God call you the apple of His eye? Have you ever seen the person He meant you to be? Do you feel cherished in spite of everything?

The Shadow of His Wings

The same confidence was claimed in the further metaphor David used: the shadow of the Lord's wings. The protecting love of the eagle for the little eaglet is implied. As Moses observed, the Lord hovers over us and guards us from that which would debilitate us in realizing the full potential we talked about in the previous chapter. The everlasting arms are beneath, above, and around us, as the hymn says so well: "In His arms He'll take and shield you; take it to the Lord in prayer."

With that quality of trust we can make it through the dark night of the soul, when we ache inside because of what people say to or about us. David felt loved and comforted as he fell asleep that night when he prayed Psalm 17. Just before he accepted the gift of renewing sleep, he said, "As for me, I will see Your face in righteousness;/I shall be satisfied when I awake in Your likeness" (v. 15). Some suggest he meant death and awaking to eternal life in God's likeness. Perhaps, but resting in the Lord's lovingkindness makes our sleep a surrender of our hurts to the Lord and awakening to a new day and a new beginning in the adventure of becoming more like our Lord.

Where Apples and Wings Meet

In a profound and renewed sense, Jesus Christ is the manifestation of both the apple of God's eye and the shadow of His wings. In Christ we experience healing love and forgiveness, but we also behold what we can become when He fills us with His Spirit. He is the love of God's protecting arms shadowing and sustaining us. He took all our hurts upon Himself at Calvary, and He rose and returned to be our never-forsaking Friend.

He says to us, "Give Me your hurts. Allow Me to love you. Deeper than your hurt is your need to trust Me. Then I will love through you the very people who have hurt you. I will give you the freedom to forgive them and depend less on their opinions and more on My faithfulness."

That's it! We are liberated from nursing our bruised feelings as soon as we tell the Lord about them and receive the courage to forgive. We awake in His likeness. Suddenly we understand that people who put us down to boost themselves can't change what they say until the Lord changes what they are.

Melville, in *Moby Dick*, puts it colorfully:

On the starboard hand of every woe, there is a sure delight; and higher the top of that delight, than the bottom of the woe is deep. . . . Delight is to Him whose strong arms yet support him, when the ship of this base treacherous world has gone down beneath him. . . . Delight—top-gallant delight—is to him who acknowledges no law or lord, but the Lord his God, and is only patriot to heaven. Delight is to him, whom all the waves and billows of the seas of the boisterous mob can never shake from the sure keel of the ages."[2]

When we listen to the Lord for what he says to us about what people have said to us, we will depend less on them and more on Him for our self-esteem. His approval releases us from clutching to people's opinions. More than longing to be liked we will be liberated to love.

4

A Seven-day Experiment in Trust
Psalm 23

So often when I complete a deep time of conversation and prayer with people who come to me for help, they will ask, "Is there something I can read to reaffirm my trust in the Lord for this problem I've just surrendered to Him?"

My response is to suggest a daily reading of the twenty-third psalm. I share with them seven powerful trust-truths contained in the psalm, one for each day of the week. Most people say, "Would you write those down for me so I can remember them?" I do that gladly, then suggest that each should be the thought for one day. The whole psalm should be reread each day and the particular verse memorized, along with the thought conditioner claiming the promise the verse offers.

A Personal Psalm

Because the twenty-third psalm uses the personal singular pronoun, I write the daily assurances in the same way. That's not to overlook the corporate experience of God's grace He wants to give to the mutually supportive fellowship of the church; but most of us start with our own needs. Believing that God knows and cares about us and will help us is difficult for many of us. Only after we experience the Lord's power are we freed to become channels of His grace to others who may be facing some of the problems we have gone through.

Here's what I give as a seven-day prescription for learning how to trust the Lord with our fears and anxieties wrapped up in the problems we face. Memorizing them, praying them each day, will make them a part of the fabric of your thinking and feeling.

First Day: *The Lord Will Work for Me!*
               "The LORD is my shepherd;/I shall not want."
Second Day: *The Lord Will Provide for Me!*
               "He makes me to lie down in green pastures;
               He leads me beside the still waters."
Third Day;   *The Lord Will Keep Me Going!*
               "He restores my soul."
Fourth Day: *The Lord Will Guide Me!*
               "He leads me in the paths of righteousness
               For His name's sake."
Fifth Day: *The Lord Will Protect Me!*
               "Yea, though I walk through the valley of the
               shadow of death,/I will fear no evil;
               For You are with me;/Your rod and Your staff, they
               comfort me."
Sixth Day: *The Lord Will Heal Me!*
               "You prepare a table before me/in the presence of
               my enemies;/You anoint my head with oil;/My
               cup runs over."
Seventh Day: *The Lord Will Pursue Me!*
               "Surely goodness and mercy shall follow me/All
               the days of my life;/And I will dwell in the house
               of the LORD/Forever."

The people who have tried this "seven days to freedom from fear" experiment have found it liberating. They begin the day reading the whole psalm, memorizing the day's verse, and repeating the day's "confidence conditioner." Then all through the day they reclaim the promise. By the end of the week they have memorized the whole psalm. Many of them repeat it at the beginning of every day after that.

Scripture is like food: It must be chewed over, swallowed, and digested for its potency to permeate our thinking and reactions. I am delighted that so many people who have tried this experiment have gone on to follow the same plan with other psalms and portions of the Old and New Testaments. Some now know great portions of Scripture to call to mind in times of need and in communicating hope to others.

The Sevenfold Promise

Now let's take these seven amazing and comforting promises as the progression of thought about this beloved psalm. David, the shepherd-king of Israel, prayed these words to his Lord, who had been to him the best of what a shepherd is to his sheep—and so much more! The psalm is rich with imagery about sheep husbandry, and some of the verses yield an even deeper meaning when we understand how a shepherd cares for his sheep. Yet we cannot read this psalm without focusing in our mind's eye Jesus Christ, who boldly said, "I am the good shepherd" (John 10:11). He is the revelation of the shepherd heart of God, and now, as resurrected, reigning Lord, He is with us as the "Great Shepherd of the sheep." Therefore, our exposition will be in that comforting context.

1. *The Lord will work for us.* Does that assertion strike you as audacious? Perhaps, but it's true. The secret of life in Christ is not our work for Him, but the work He does in us, through us, and for us. Nothing sets us free from fear any more than knowing that at this moment, during this day, and in the projects and problems that confront us, our Shepherd is constantly working for our welfare.

We need not want. Like the shepherd who is constantly thinking ahead for places for his sheep to graze and have their thirst quenched, our Good Shepherd knows what we need before we ask Him and is persistently moving out ahead of us, preparing exactly what we need, when we need it. The Good Shepherd, the eternal *Logos* ("Word") who hung the stars, cares about our hang-ups.

Why, then, are we still anxious and filled with worry? We stray from the flock, resist the plans our Shepherd has made, and think we can find better pastures on our own. Sheep have a will of their own; so do we. Worry never changed anything except the worrier! Worry prompts us to take things into our own hands and try to work them out for ourselves. Also, we labor with the misapprehension that we are to strive to work for the Lord to be accepted and approved by Him.

That distortion has been around for a long time, the old justification by works idea that gave wings to the "God helps those who help themselves" heresy. We were meant to be recipients of the Lord's wisdom for our thinking, His love for our relationships, and His strength for our bodies. Life in the flow of His Spirit is one in which we depend on Him to work within us and arrange circumstances around us.

That makes life a succession of surprises. We work, to be sure, but with His power and His might. And we will be amazed constantly at what unpredictable things He has prepared for us. We can invest ourselves energetically to use the thoughts, strength, and opportunities He's provided.

I like the story of the little boy who got the wording of the first verse of the twenty-third psalm mixed up. "The Lord is my shepherd; I don't want anything else." The wording may have been rearranged, but the true meaning was expressed splendidly! That expression of ultimate trust comes when we have a personal relationship with our Shepherd and really trust Him to work for us.

Two men repeated the Shepherd's Psalm in a church service. One was a great actor, and he repeated it with magnificent eloquence. Then a little old man walked down the aisle of the congregation, up onto the platform, leaned on his cane, and began to repeat the words from memory. A silence came over the entire congregation. They had clapped for the great actor, but for the little old man, there was silence. The actor, expressing his maturity, got up and said, "I know the shepherd psalm, but this great man knows the Shepherd."

Martin Luther said that great religion and faith is expressed in personal pronouns. When we can say, "The Lord is *my* shepherd," we can affirm, "I shall not want." When we move from the vagueness of generalities, from cultural or religious ideas, or from creeds, rites, or rituals, into that dynamic, personal relationship for which we were born as the sheep of the Lord, then we can say, "There's nothing I want," or with the little boy, "I don't want anything else." Have you ever said that? "Lord, I need you more than I need any gift You can give me, any answer to prayer that You can provide, any solution to any problem that You can offer. Lord, I want *You*. I need You to be my shepherd." Can you say that? Have you said it? Say it right now.

2. Not only will the Lord work for us, but *the Lord will provide for us*. He leads us day by day into exactly what we need. Green pastures and still waters describe what the sheep need. They are grazing areas that provide exactly the kind of food that the sheep need at a particular time. Sheep will usually not lie down until they are fed and satisfied and have no fear. The more I study sheep husbandry, the more I understand that you can't make a sheep lie down, you can't kick it down, you can't push it down, you can't press it down, unless some basic needs have been cared for.

First, a sheep must be free of fear. Second, its coat must be cleared of any of the parasites that would disturb it if it were to rest in the green grass. Third, a sheep will not lie down while it is still hungry. Only contented sheep lie down. That's why David, in declaring his own faith, "He makes me to lie down in green pastures," is really saying, "He has fed me with exactly what I need at this moment." But fourth and most important of all, a sheep will not lie down without the knowledge of the presence of the shepherd.

Still water is very important to a sheep. A sheep will not go close to running, fast-moving water. If it fell or was pushed into the water, its heavy coat of wool would soon be saturated and it would drown. Sheep have learned to fear rushing, gushing, moving water and to search for quiet pools from which to drink. The shepherd knows this and is in constant search of the quiet watering places where his sheep may be replenished so that they will be able to rest.

3. *The Lord will keep us going.* That's what David meant when he said, "He restores my soul" (v. 3).

We need to understand something about downcast sheep. Are you ever downcast? That term comes from sheep husbandry. A *cast* sheep is one that has rested in the green grass next to a hollow in the ground and, as a result of the force of gravity, has rolled over on its back. A sheep that is covered with heavy wool, or is fat, or has gotten into a position where it cannot avoid the rolling-over danger, has become a cast sheep. From that image comes the idea of downcast. *Downcast* is being in a condition in which you can't roll back onto your feet.

Now, putting a sheep back on its feet is a tender process that must be done in just the right way. The shepherd must take the sheep and lift it up. Since being on its back has caused the blood to drain from its legs and feet, the shepherd must rub the legs until the sheep is able to stand. The shepherd knows the right moment that he can let go of the sheep. What does that mean to us? The Lord will get us back on our feet!

I remember calling on a woman in the hospital. She was a downcast person. For the first time in her life, her smooth exterior had been penetrated with the realization of what her attitudes had done to her family. She felt herself to be a failure and feared the future for her children. In one unguarded moment of expressing her fears, she began to hit herself with her hands and kick her feet against the bed. Suddenly, she realized what she had done. She was like a downcast sheep, kicking frantically, crying out for help. I was able to explain to her how a good shepherd helps the sheep and gets it back on its feet again. I told her about the Lord's forgiveness and acceptance, and how He takes us where we are and gives us a new beginning. By the end of that long conversation, she was able to repeat the psalm after me. Then I explained salvation and introduced her to the Good Shepherd.

David knew how the Lord takes care of downcast people. I believe he wrote this magnificent shepherd's psalm later in his life when he could look back and remember all the times that he had been on his back, unable to move because he was paralyzed by the failures of his life. Each time, the Lord restored his soul. In using the word *soul*, David was referring to his whole being, his life. The Lord restores *me!* Have you ever been restored by Him when you've been downcast? The Lord wants to get us on our feet, get us going again, and keep us going. How will He do that?

4. *The Lord will guide us.* " . . . He leads me in the paths of righteousness/For His name's sake" (v. 3). The words are filled with majestic meaning. Righteousness, as we will discuss at length in a subsequent chapter, is a right relationship with the Lord, based on accepting His love and forgiveness as a gift of grace. He provides us with the capacity of faith to respond to complete justification made possible through the blood of the cross. We don't deserve it; we can't earn it. We have that status because He has declared us forgiven, accepted, and cherished for eternity. He will not turn away from us or let us go.

We often try to negate that status, however, by seeking to justify ourselves by goodness, hard work, or efforts to earn what is ours already. We long for our Good Shepherd to lead us away from those dead-end paths. We need to pray, "Lord, lead me away from the self-defeating patterns of willfulness that tie me up in knots. Keep me from bashing down locked doors while the door You've opened for me stands open, ready for me to go through!"

This reassuring verse of the psalm also means that we can depend on the Lord to guide decisions that will keep us in the center of His will. He uses our prayers, guides our thinking, leads us to clarifying Scripture, communicates through people, and utilizes circumstances to help us be sure in each crucial decision. Our task is to surrender our decisions before they must be made, give ourselves adequate time for Him to condition our thinking and liberate our wills, and then we can be sure He will use everything at His disposal to show us the path that not only is right, but will help us grow in the realization of our righteousness in Him.

5. *The Lord will also protect us.* "Yea, though I walk through the

valley of the shadow of death,/I will fear no evil:/For You are with me;/Your rod and Your staff, they comfort me" (v. 4).

The valley of the shadow of death might be rendered "the glen of deep gloom." David used a familiar Hebrew term here in describing the vicissitudes of walking in a dangerous place, through a difficult experience, or even facing death itself. A portion of that road from Jerusalem to the Dead Sea was called the Valley of the Shadow. Even there, his shepherd would be with him. The enemies that might attack would be overcome. He had known that in a multitude of battles all through his life. The way he had cared for his sheep as a shepherd boy in Judea was an example for him of the way the Lord, in a so much greater way, would continue to care for him.

The protecting care of the shepherd was symbolized by his rod and staff. The rod was taken from the lower trunk and upper roots of a sapling, including the roundness of where the roots were connected to the trunk. Therefore, at the end of the rod there was a gnarled ball that made the three- to four-foot rod a powerful weapon. A shepherd learned to throw it with deadly accuracy and could also use it to beat off attackers.

The shepherd's staff had a crook on the end of it. It was used not only to reach out to get hold of a wandering sheep, but to keep the sheep together. Interestingly, a shepherd handled a new lamb by the crook because if he touched it with his hands, the smell of his hands would make the mother reject the lamb. The staff was the instrument of tender care. For David, it meant the Lord's protection and His grace. For us, it is a further sign of the fact that when we are open to His direction, He guides and surrounds us with protecting care each step of the way, in any period of life that may be filled with fear.

The phrase, "You prepare a table before me in the presence of my enemies" (v. 5), is filled with meaning, not only because of the activities of a shepherd, but also because of the nomadic customs of that time. For the shepherd, the table meant those grazing lands high in the mountains that could be reached only after the snow receded. The shepherd carefully prepared the grazing area. He went before the sheep and on his hands and knees went through the grass, pulling out any of the noxious weeds, briars, or thorny growths that would eventually cause difficulty for the sheep. No effort was spared.

Do you see the connection with Holy Communion here?

David also knew of the custom that a person could not be attacked while eating in another man's tent. If you could reach a friend's tent—even though your enemies were in hot pursuit—you were safe at his table. The Lord feeds us with His grace and holds off the enemies of life—the enemies of our soul, the things that cause us to be afraid, frustrated, and anxious.

6. *The Lord will heal us.* The healing ministry of the shepherd for the sheep was a very important one. As a matter of fact, I learned of a blind shepherd who knew the faces of all his sheep by the touch of his hand. Can you feel the Lord's hand upon your face, knowing you as unique and special, the recipient of His loving care?

The anointing oil of the shepherd was made up of olive oil, sulphur, and spices to keep off the gnats and flies and insects, and to penetrate the cuts and bruises on the face of the sheep. *Anointing* in the Hebrew-Christian tradition means the blessing of the Lord, the healing of the Lord, the appointment of the Lord, and the joy of the Lord. To be anointed by Him is to have Him place His loving hand upon us and fill us with His Spirit.

Cup is the portion—literally in Hebrew, "my life." God makes our lives overflow. When He anoints us with the oil of His healing, our inner heart is filled with a joy that we cannot contain.

7. *The Lord pursues us.* In every situation He will invade our needs with mercy and goodness.

The word for *follow* used here is to *pursue.* Just as the shepherd's dogs followed the flock, keeping them together with their watchful care, the Lord will come to us with "goodness and mercy" in those times when we are afraid.

The goodness of the Lord includes His consistency. He cannot be other than He is—a forgiving, accepting, caring Friend who knows our needs and comes to us, pursuing us in spite of our rejection of Him, using everything to keep us close to Him and His flock. His mercy and His grace are the expressions of forgiveness given before we ask, bathing the hurting places of our heart with tenderness. The Lord changes our turbulent, timorous emotions with the assurance that He will be with us in spite of everything.

He will never let us go. David wrote confidently, "I will dwell in the house of the Lord forever" (v. 6). Jesus said, "'In My Father's house are many mansions'" (John 14:2). The word really means abiding places or abodes, promising not only eternal security but our relationship with the Lord now. There are many times when we cry out, "Lord, help me!" and He's with us. He gives us exactly what we need—a place in His heart and an assurance that not even death can separate us from Him. We are alive forever!

A dear Scottish friend of mine gave me a statue of Sir Harry Lauder which always reminds me of one of the great stories of Lauder. One time he was in Chicago to sing just after he had lost his son in an untimely death.

Filled with new trust in the Lord for His comfort and care, Sir Harry Lauder sang with joy and peace that radiated out to the audience. When he finished, people gave him a standing ovation. They would not stop clapping. Finally, after several curtain calls, he stopped the thunderous applause and said, "Don't thank me; thank the good Lord, the Shepherd of my life, for He put the song in my heart."

Sing your song, sing the song of your Shepherd. He'll work for you; He'll provide for you; He'll guide you; He'll protect you; He'll heal you.

He'll pursue you and never let you go. The Lord is my Shepherd. Is He yours?

Yes, He is. Claim His love. Trust Him. Praying the Shepherd's Psalm daily, kneading it into your heart with memorization and reiterating its promises all through your days, will set you free to live with freedom from fear this week, and forever.

5

You Don't Need More Faith!
Psalm 27

My time for quiet study in a New York hotel room before giving a speech was suddenly interrupted. The undeniable ring of the fire alarm jarred me from my chair. I quickly checked the map on the door for escape routes. As I was about to leave my room for the nearest stairway, a blaring announcement was made on a public address speaker in the corridor. The words of a much too panicky voice gave clear instructions but little comfort.

"Please return and stay in your room. Close your door and wait for further instructions. Thank you. Please be calm. Please be calm."

Be calm? That was not easy. I pictured the worst. The hotel, I had learned earlier in the day from a much too talkative doorman, had been under the siege of an arsonist who had kept the management under constant alert and jangled nerves by repeatedly setting off fire alarms. Was this another false alarm or the real thing?

All I had to go on was the message of the woman on the intercom. "Stay where you are. Wait. Be calm." The instructions were repeated often as the minutes of what seemed to be an endless waiting period ticked by.

As I sat there in my room I reflected on how difficult it is to wait for the solution to life's problems. Waiting is not easy for any of us.

I'm happy to report that it was another false alarm. There was no fire. I returned to my preparation, later gave my speech, and left the hotel the next day. The memory of the event, however, did not leave me as easily.

The words of the frantic voice on the corridor speaker reminded me of the advice we often give to loved ones and friends when they face problems: "Wait . . . be calm . . . don't worry."

But there's a much more disturbing admonition that's often given glibly while people wait for a resolution to their problems. When the waiting period goes on longer than we or they expected, we hear, "What you need is more faith!" More *faith?* Some speak of faith as if it were something we could produce. Instead of helping people, this message drives them into a prison of self-incrimination.

The "More Faith" Heresy

Lately, I've truly become alarmed at the distressing proportion of this heresy among Christians. We put others and ourselves under tremendous pressure by demanding that we should have more faith. Lack of faith is used as an explanation for why problems are not solved, broken relationships are not healed, and sicknesses persist. Demanding that we force more faith in life's problems is like telling an already healthy man to bench press fifteen hundred pounds!

One day a young man named Abraham Lincoln saw the terrible consequences of the slave trade. The dehumanization of human beings enslaved by others cut to the core of his indignation. He said, "If I ever get a chance, I'm going to hit this thing and hit it hard!"

I have the same feeling about the way we incarcerate people by telling them that the reason their problems are not solved is that they don't have enough faith. We make them indentured servants with a price tag on their freedom that they can never pay. Our "solution" is a denial of God, the gospel, and the relationship out of which faith is entrusted to us.

I meet people everywhere who are suffering because of this heresy. They have been victims of those around them who wanted to provide an easy, quick, and simplistic solution to the problems.

When the problems persist, there seems to be only one explanation: They didn't have enough faith!

This cultic phenomenon got to me one day recently on a personal level. Perhaps I was so alarmed because it all happened in one day. Everyone I talked to was facing problems, and each, in various ways, confessed the same need. All wanted more faith in order to endure the problems.

A woman said, "This probably wouldn't have happened if I had had more faith!" A man exclaimed, "If I only had more faith I could lick this!" A teen-ager ill in the hospital explained his lack of progress with the self-incriminating, "Well, I guess I don't have enough faith," and a television viewer who wrote me multiplied her marital problems by lambasting her own deficiency of trust: "I know my husband would change if I had a deeper faith."

We all have problems, some more serious than others. There are times when problems pile up and our backs are against the wall. Sooner or later, we cry out to God for help. When the answer does not come when we want it or in the way we prescribed, we cast about for explanations. At that point we turn inwardly and wonder what's wrong with us. Most of us have been raised with the idea that faith is something we must produce before God will act. Therefore, if He does not act immediately we diagnose the difficulty as our lack of faith.

Such a belief exposes a profound misunderstanding of God as well as the nature of faith. If God is all knowing, all powerful, and all loving, would He wait for us to conjure up the right qualifications? More than that, the Bible is undeniably clear that faith is a gift, not something we produce. Faith is a gift from God to us. The quality of our faith is not what prompts God to act. Faith does not produce an intimate relationship with God; an intimate relationship with God issues in faith. Faith is the outer manifestation of an inner heart in communion with God. The more of Him that dwells in our hearts, the more faith we will have for our problems. Faith is our response to the loving presence of a God who comes to us in our problems.

When problems pile up, our need is not to have more faith to get God to solve them, but to seek God for Himself. Problems are an alarm signal of our need for Him. When we are distressed and cast desperately about for faith to endure, we miss the end by focusing on the means. God is the source and end—"the author and finisher"—of faith.

Our quest for faith is often a substitute for communion with Christ. You and I don't need more faith; we need more of God! Instead of longing for more faith to get more from God, we need to get more of God into us. When problems cause panic, it is a sure sign that our hearts need God rather than more faith.

The Psalm of Faith

In times of problems, I turn to the twenty-seventh psalm. The reason is that I, like most of us, have the tendency to blame myself for my problems and then complicate the problems by accusing myself of not having enough faith to solve them. I end up with a bigger mess than when I started. The problems are bad enough; thinking I could solve them with more faith drives me further from God and deeper into panic.

In Psalm 27, the psalmist teaches me what to do when life dishes out more problems than I can take. The psalmist's first response when faced with dangers and difficulties was not to list what he needed to get God's help, but instead to describe what God could give him to face his need. His problems were like a dinner bell, alerting him to the realization of his hunger and thirst for the living God.

Psalm 27 is divided into two parts: Verses 1–6 show how the psalmist comes to grips with his problems and realizes his need for God; verses 7–14 reveal the content of his communion with God and the gift of faith that results. Some expositors have suggested that Psalm 27 might be made up of two different psalms, written by two different people at two very different times and in very contrasting circumstances. But my conviction is that there is an inherent unity in the psalm, and taken as a whole it gives us a progression of what to think, say, do, and be when we are encumbered with problems. Thus, there are four very natural divisions: (1) what the psalmist thought to himself; (2) what he said to God; (3) what God said to him; and finally, (4) what he said to himself as a result.

The key word in the Psalm is *heart*. The Hebrew understanding of heart included intellect, emotion, and will. The psalmist's heart was troubled by the dangers around him because of his enemies. In this magnificent psalm we witness a human heart as it experiences first panic, then perspective, then power, and ultimately, the gift of peace through faith in the goodness of God.

We all long for the faith the psalmist had at the end of the psalm. He was determined to wait on the Lord, to trust His timing, and to quietly expect His intervention. What we need to experience, however, are the steps he went through to arrive at that sublime staying power of endurance. We can experience that if we say and do what he did. The gift of faith will be given, courage will be engendered, and endurance will result.

What the Psalmist Thought

Consider first what the psalmist thought when problems besieged him on every side. He thought more about God than he thought about the problems!

His first idea was not whether he could take the problems but the triumphant adequacy of God. Proverbs tells us that as a person "thinks in his heart, so is he" (23:7). I would add, "What a person thinks about God will determine what he does about his problem."

We are tempted to become so focused on the problems that we miss the power available to help us solve them. Inevitably, then, we focus on the inadequacy of our faith. That's when the panic sets in.

We cry out, "What am I going to do?" instead of "What is God able to do?" We are tempted to think our problems are bigger than God. The result is that we pray to the problems rather than to God.

Note carefully, then, what the psalmist thought about in the midst of his problems. He thought first about God and his need for Him. His thoughts focused on the guidance, deliverance, strength, and protection of God.

> The LORD is my light and my salvation;
> Whom shall I fear?
> The Lord is the strength of my life;
> Of whom shall I be afraid?
> . . . Though an army shall encamp against me,
> My heart shall not fear;
> Though war should rise against me,
> In this I will be confident (vv. 1, 3).

What the psalmist needed in his problems, only God could give him. He needed light in the darkness. God doesn't give the light of His guidance apart from Himself. He *is* light—intellectual, emotional, volitional light. He shows us what to do and gives us the inclination and the will to attempt it.

Salvation here simply means deliverance, a way out of what seem to be insolvable problems.

Those of us who read the psalm through the focus of Calvary see so much more in those words. God our light has come to us in the One who said, "'I am the light of the world'" (John 8:12) and, "'. . . In this world you will have tribulation; but be of good cheer, I have overcome the world'" (John 16:33). The light and salvation of God revealed in Jesus Christ are two parts of His gift. Christ's light exposes God's heart and illuminates our sin. His death on the cross assures us of undying love and unlimited forgiveness.

Added to that, we know that as He delivered us from the power of evil and death, He intervenes in each of our problems to give us exactly what we need in a way and at a time that's His best for us.

What the Psalmist Said

Why then, is it so difficult to say what the psalmist said, "My heart shall not fear" (v. 3)? What God had done for him previously had taught him a great lesson. In his problems, his confidence led to one dominant desire—a heart longing to be with Him. "One thing I have desired of the LORD,/That will I seek:/That I may dwell in the house of the LORD/All the days of my life . . ." (v. 4).

Problems drive some of us away from God. We blame Him for them or wonder how He could allow them if He loves us. Not so with the psalmist. The magnitude of his problems led him to the momentous loneliness he felt for God. He longed to behold the beauty of the Lord in His temple, to be hidden in His pavilion, to find safety in the secret place of His tabernacle, and to be set above his enemies on a solid rock away from their reach (see vv. 4–5).

What this says to you and me in the midst of our perplexities is that meditation about God leads us to the desire to be with God. We can thank Him for life's problems if they have led us to think more about Him and if our meditation about Him has prompted the desire to be with Him.

What God Said to the Psalmist

Now we are ready to hear what the Lord said to the psalmist when problems led him to cry out to God. There is one statement God always makes when we come to Him with our problems. He doesn't always give us a solution immediately, nor does He check us out to see if we have enough faith. Usually we are so battered and buffeted by the problems that there is little to offer Him except our need. His admonition is, "Seek My face" (v. 8).

The psalmist responded in a way that exemplifies the one thing we can do to find help in our time of need. ". . . My heart said to

You, 'Your face, LORD, I will seek'" (v. 8). In Hebrew, a single word means both *face* and *presence*. The Lord promised Moses, ". . . 'My Presence will go with you, and I will give you rest'" (Ex. 33:14). Then Moses said to the Lord what we all want to say about the impossibility of facing our problems alone. ". . . 'If Your Presence does not go with us, do not bring us up from here'"! (v. 15).

For us, the face of God is known in His incarnate portrait. We say with Paul, "For it is the God who commanded light to shine out of darkness who has shone in our hearts to give the light of the knowledge of the glory of God in the face of Jesus Christ" (2 Cor. 4:6). The same God who created the universe, who called and guided the people of Israel by a pillar of cloud by day and fire by night, who came in Jesus Christ to save us, is also present with us in the Person of the Holy Spirit. We are not alone in our problems. The face of Jesus Christ leads us into the glory of God the Father and on to the grace of His Holy Spirit.

There is no better advice in our problems than "Seek My face." The words mean "Seek Me; in Me is your comfort, your protection, your guidance, your safety." The more we seek His face, the more we can face our problems! In His presence we are given love and acceptance. New and proper self-esteem grows. We realize that we belong to the Lord and not to the problems. Our one great problem of where we will spend eternity is settled, and that settles our nerves to see our temporary problems for what they are.

So when we or the people around us are deeply enmeshed in problems, the first encouragement should be to seek God's face by spending time in consistent, habitual prayer—not only talking to God, but also listening to Him. The desire to pray is always the result of God's prior desire to talk to us. He calls us before we call on Him. He is constantly sounding the invitation to seek His face. When problems mount, listen! In your soul you'll hear the call, "Seek My face." And the response of our eager hearts will be, "Your face, Lord, I will seek."

In face to face communion, the Lord tells us of His love and care. His word is grace. He leads us to Calvary to receive the forgiveness and acceptance of His death for us, then to an open tomb to remind us of His intervening, victorious power, and then on to an upper room to hear of His indwelling presence. He says, "Beloved, do not panic in your problems. We will confront them together. I will give you exactly what you need." Suddenly, a mysterious capacity grows within us. We have faith to endure.

What the Psalmist Told Himself

Lastly, note the result of what the psalmist said to himself after listening to God.

> I would have lost heart, unless I had believed
> That I would see the goodness of the LORD
> In the land of the living.
> Wait on the LORD;
> Be of good courage,
> And He shall strengthen your heart;
> Wait, I say, on the LORD! (vv. 13–14).

Now that's the outward expression in words of the inner gift of faith. Problems have shrunk to their impotent size. They no longer possess us but we have the daring to possess them.

Paul has given us the progression of how this works when we are face to face with the Lord. Let's look at Romans 5:1–5 to see what the gift of faith does for us in our problems.

> Therefore, having been justified by faith, we have peace with God through our Lord Jesus Christ, through whom also we have access by faith into this grace in which we stand, and rejoice in hope of the glory of God. And not only that, but we also glory in tribulations, knowing that tribulation produces perseverance; and perseverance, character; and character, hope. Now hope does not disappoint, because the love of God has been poured out in our hearts by the Holy Spirit who was given to us.

Faith makes us right with God and makes us capable of facing our problems with staying power. But before we leap to the self-justifying impulse to try to manufacture that quality of faith, we need to hear Paul again. "For by grace you have been saved through faith, and that not of yourselves; it is a gift of God, not of works, lest anyone should boast" (Eph. 2:8–9). This faith, which God gives us to reach out and accept His grace through Christ, cannot be earned, deserved, or acquired by effort. The Lord gives it to those who respond to His call to seek His face.

Added to this basic faith, the Holy Spirit in us engenders an advanced faith to trust Him in specific problems. This is "the grace in which we stand" when others fall and life crumbles about us. But there is more! This faith He provides becomes the rock. Remember Jesus' words to Peter, "'. . . You are Peter, and on this rock I will build My church, and the gates of Hades shall not prevail against it'" (Matt. 16:18). Simon's new name meant rock. What was the rock? Faith! The Lord did not build His church on Peter apart from his rock-like faith.

In that light, look again to Paul's words. With faith we can glory in our problems, knowing that they produce perseverance, the realization of specific confidence in the Lord's power. That kindles the growth in Christlike character that issues hope. With hope we can wait for the Lord's timely resolution of some problems, and an on-time flow of endurance for others. Endurance is the Lord's Spirit in us. He pours Himself into us so we can go back into our problems as courageous people. We can wait for the promise that we will be repeatedly filled with the Holy Spirit, not once, but daily. With each problem we will be given power.

My dear friend Louise Mohr discovered this recently. She is one of the truly great women who has helped thousands in their need. Her earthy, unpious, sometimes gutsy explanation of the abundant life has reached many who have been turned off by traditional religion. Now she needed the Lord's enduring courage herself.

After a long illness, her beloved husband, Sidney, died. While she was recovering from that loss, her eyesight began to fail. The surgeon told her that he could not remedy the disability with further surgery. Added to that, she was hit with deep concern for a loved one. Problems piled up.

One day she sat down to write God a letter. In her customary frankness, she told God what she thought about the whole mess and signed her name. Real prayer isn't always lofty rhetoric on our knees. Sometimes it's a one- or two-word expression of exasperation.

The next day Louise saw her next-door neighbor. In response to a neighborly, "How's it going?" she relayed some of the problems and shared that she had told God in very clear terms how she was feeling. She told her neighbor about her letter to Him. A couple of days later, my friend received a letter:

Dear Louise:
  You think you've got problems! I've got a whole universe to run, with people who have problems as big or bigger than yours. But I know and care about you. I will give you what you need to endure. You will have faith to trust Me!

Love,
God.

That sensitive neighbor had a sense of humor and a sense of empathy. She had written the letter. It was just what Louise needed: a reminder from the Lord, through a friend, that His grace was sufficient.

The Lord does get through to us. He will use any and all means to bring us back to face-to-face communion. Because Louise was in that frank and honest friendship with the Master, she could tell Him how she felt. He heard and responded with His Spirit's staying power. She can wait on the Lord, in spite of everything! I am so thankful that neighbor didn't dismiss her with a saccharine, "Just have faith." Instead, in an imaginative way, she reminded my friend that she was loved and that the Lord would not forsake her.

Part of the Process

Problems are part of the process of life, and the process is the product. Thinking that we will arrive at some blessed plateau where all our problems will be gone is a mistake. There are always more than enough dilemmas to go around. Even when we get on top of our troubles for a time, there are people all around us with more than they can handle, who need our help. The secret is to face the problems that come as an opportunity to receive more of the power the Lord is ready to give.

We can thank God for problems because they are opportunities to cooperate with Him in His continuing creation. Problems bring us to a realization of how much we need Him.

John Wesley had always thought he had faith until the time he was on board a ship returning to England from missionary work in America. The ship was caught in a violent storm. Fear gripped him. He observed that the only people on the ship who were not filled with terror were a band of Moravian missionaries.

After the storm, Wesley asked one of them, "Were you not afraid?"

"Afraid?" responded the Moravian. "Why should I be afraid? I know Christ!"

And then with disturbing frankness he asked Wesley, "Do you know Christ?"

For the first time Wesley realized that he did not. He had been trained as a clergyman, educated at Oxford, and was ordained to the ministry, but he had only a vague knowledge of the Lord. The shattering realization prepared the way for Wesley later to meet Christ personally when his heart was "strangely warmed" by face-to-face communion. His insecure, secondhand religion was replaced by the gift of faith which enabled him to endure.

Problems can do that. When we meet people who are vibrant with faith we feel our need. We say,

> . . . that I could think there trembled through
> His happy good-night air
> Some blessed Hope, whereof he knew
> And I was unaware.[1]

The Lord wants to give us the blessed privilege of being able to say with Bernard of Clairvaux,

> Ah this,
> Nor tongue nor pen can show;
> The love of Jesus what it is
> None but His loved ones know.

In our problems the Lord's gracious word is "Come!" We can come to Him because He has come to us first, to give us the dominant desire for Him rather than simply an escape from our problems.

Thomas à Kempis in *The Imitation of Christ* prayed, "It is too small and unsatisfactory whatever Thou bestowest on me, apart from Thyself."[2]

George Matheson sounds the same note in his prayer: "Whether Thou comest in sunshine or rain, I would take Thee into my heart joyfully. Thou art Thyself compensation for the rain. It is Thee and not Thy gifts I crave."[3]

There's a lovely story of Michelangelo that illustrates what happens to us when the Lord hides us in the tabernacle of intimate prayer. A great piece of marble resisted the artistry of many sculptors. When Michelangelo was asked to try his hand, he insisted that a temporary booth be erected over the marble and that he be left alone with the marble. After a long time the master artist emerged and asked that the makeshift pavilion be removed. When it was dismantled, there was David!

That's how the Lord sculpts the person He wants us to be. In the quiet seclusion, alone with us, He makes our face like His own—a face radiant with strong, enduring courage because our hearts are filled with Him.

What we need to face life's problems has been given. We have faith. Tribulation has produced perseverance, character, and hope. And beyond that, expectation—not of what we will do to solve our problems, but of what the Lord will do. Mysteriously, we are able to say, "Wait on the Lord! I want only what He wills . . . and when He wills it."

6

When God Seems Absent
Psalm 42

Some months ago, I attended a very turbulent meeting, filled with conflict and misunderstanding. When the vote was taken on the issue confronting the meeting, not everyone agreed.

The one who objected most of all was the secretary of the meeting. He didn't believe that what was decided was in keeping with what God wanted. The man did have the final word, however, when he sent out the minutes of the meeting. He listed all those who were present. Then, in the place he usually listed those who were absent, he recorded one absentee: God!

The secretary's analysis was that God had been absent from the meeting, so there had been conflict, confusion—and the secretary hadn't had his way in the vote that was taken on the resolution. Listing God as absent was presumptuous, of course, and a childish way of registering his disgruntled feelings. But the secretary did make his point.

God's Absence: Fact or Feeling?

Have you ever felt that what happened to you or around you could never have occurred if God had been present? Have you ever wanted to write the minutes of some experience or portion of your life the way that secretary did? *Absent: God.* And what about the things people do? Have you ever wanted to say, "How could God allow that person to get away with it? Doesn't He care? He must not have been there!" Or think of life's difficult circumstances, contra-dictions, or injustices. How can God be present and allow such things to exist?

The feeling of the absence of God is one that we've all had at times. That experience is most poignant in our personal spiritual lives. We know times of great joy and companionship with God, then suddenly, life changes. We are faced with new challenges, difficult surroundings, new people, and problems we've not dealt with before. Only then do we realize that our experience of God has been dependent on sameness, familiar surroundings, and a carefully ordered life.

Yet, there are also times when the strange feeling of the absence of God comes over us when there is no logical explanation. One of the most important discoveries in living is that the feeling of God's absence may actually be our emotional response to His presence manifested in a new way, demanding new growth and maturity in our relationship with Him.

I want to investigate this mysterious reality of the spiritual life with you in this chapter. I've never talked to a truly great Christian who hasn't at some time had the feeling that the Lord may have withdrawn His blessing. The experience usually has contributed to his or her greatness. He or she depended less on feelings and more on the faithfulness of the Lord.

The Psalm Where God Showed Up

The psalmist went through a time when God seemed absent. He expressed it with poignant clarity in the forty-second psalm. Through the experience, he found that God could be depended on as an ultimately reliable source of hope.

Some geographical and historical background will help. The psalmist was in the region of Mount Hermon, far to the north of Jerusalem and all the customary practices of the temple. His refer-ences in verse 6 and 7 establish that. There at the foot of Mount

Hermon, the metaphor of God's might in the past, and at the head-waters of the River Jordan, the psalmist longed to be back in Jerusalem. He remembered the joyous processions to the temple, the feasts and festivals, and the stirring worship of the Lord that had come to mean so much to him (see v. 4).

What was he doing away from Jerusalem? My theory is that he was probably a part of a forced march of exiles being transported away from Jerusalem into a strange and foreign land. The troubling question on his mind seemed to be, "How can I find God away from the people and the familiar surroundings of Jerusalem where I've known and loved him?" His enemies taunted him with their own question: "Where is your God?" Soon it became his own anxious query. "Indeed, where are You, God?"

He felt the panic of the thought. God seemed absent.

Finally, the psalmist could evade the question no longer. That forced him into dialogue with his own soul. "Why are you cast down, O my soul?/And why are you disquieted within me? . . ." (v. 5). Then he gave himself a stern talking-to, with a firm admonition to his soul. ". . . Hope in God, for I shall yet praise Him/For the help of His countenance" (v. 5).

Yet there was no relief until he brought his frightened feelings to God Himself—an awesome growth in his understanding of God. God was not limited to Jerusalem or the temple. He was not absent at all! "O my God, my soul is cast down within me;/Therefore, I will remember you from the land of the Jordan,/And from the heights of Hermon . . ." (v. 6). The tumbling cataracts of the waterfall reminded him of the Lord's prayer. The melting snow on the peaks of Hermon made a rushing river that flowed into the riverbed of the Jordan.

I have been to that very place and heard the waterfall and the winds howl. The psalmist knew God was there with him, and that fact freed him to praise Him where he was rather than where he had been. The experience provided an answer to the question of his disquieted soul. God had not left him. God was now more than ever the help of his countenance and his God (v. 11).

The Lord had not caused the psalmist's removal from Jerusalem, but He certainly had used it. The sure knowledge of His omnipotence could not have happened back in the security of the holy city, however often the psalmist might have read or sung Scripture that proclaimed it. An experience of what seemed to be the Lord's absence was what was necessary to really find Him, know Him, and love Him for Himself. The same is true for us.

A Chance to Grow

Consider first that the sense of the absence of God is really the chance to grow. Isaiah 45:15 puts the awesome truth bluntly: "Truly You are God, who hide Yourself. . . ." Yet look at the context. God hid Himself in judgment as the people became idolatrous in depending on false gods of security, military might, and heritage. The judgment of God often feels like His absence.

Such truth brings us closer to an understanding of the feeling that God is absent. Perhaps there are two sides to that experience. When God begins to penetrate our lives, the action often creates a feeling of His absence. We may feel as if He has removed His love. Actually, we are being introduced to a deeper love in His heart. Just as when a true friend cares enough to alert us to things we need to change, we may feel he or she has withdrawn approval. A feeling of distance results—from inside us—not from the other person who has risked to help us see ourselves as we are coming across to others. The same may be true in our relationship with God.

We are faced with a paradox. At times, the closer God gets the more we feel He is distant. He is penetrating areas of character, behavior, understanding, commitments, and values. He never leaves or forsakes us, but a temporary emotional feeling of His absence occurs when there is something in our lives that is blocking us from Him or we are unwilling to obey Him in some area of our lives. Those are times when we can learn something about Him that we've never discovered before. Praying through the forty-second psalm, making it our own plea, can set us free to grow. In the previous chapter we establ shed that we do not need more faith but deeper faith, to trust God to help us deal with the changing demands of life.

At first the psalmist wanted to go back to Jerusalem and his provincial, localized God. Eventually he became thankful that the Lord did not permit that. Instead, He gave him a fresh experience of His sovereignty and His grace, so that He could show him He was always with him to sustain him, regardless of the vicissitudes and difficulties in which he found himself. That developed muscle in the psalmist's soul. He was given the chance to experience greatness.

There's a great difference between the god of our own making, limited to past experiences of growth, and the present experience of God, the holy Lord God. Many of us cherish memories of God's previous goodness. Some of us have sentimentalized our faith, being dependent on the way we knew Him back home, at some retreat center, in some wonderfully warm experience of inspiration, or in some time of need when He intervened to help us. We need to get up-to-date with Him.

The feeling of the absence of God can be simply the flip side of God demanding to be contemporary, to be vital with us where we are. Because He forces us to let go of the ropes of security that moor us to the past, we often feel as if He's not there.

He is—be sure of that. Strange or unfamiliar circumstances have not dismissed Him. He is with us in them and will use them for our growth in greatness.

How then shall we pray? Something like this: "Dear God, I claim Your presence and power right now where I am. The contradiction of the circumstances has not changed You. Reveal more of Yourself to me. Help me to know You more intimately than ever before. I place my hope in You, not in the strange, different circumstances in which I find myself. I long to grow into the greatness You have intended for me."

A New Level of Love

Second, think about the fact that the sense of the absence of God is the prelude to an introduction to who He really is. He is the same yesterday, today, and forever. He does not change, but He longs to introduce us to deeper dimensions of His heart.

Collecting ideas about God that are not biblical or consistent with His revealed nature is easy. He must contradict those cultural, religious, or traditional ideas. When the Lord presses us into intellectual growth, we are denied our cherished ideas and rhetoric.

A woman said after a class on the cross I taught recently, "You've taken my god away!"

That alarmed me. I inquired what she meant. Smiling, she said, "Don't worry. The god I had was really no god at all. You have introduced me to the cross in the heart of God that I had never known about before. What happened on Calvary was not an afterthought. It revealed in time and space to us what God is really like.

"That has transformed my thinking and the way I pray. At first, I felt as if all I had believed before was being taken from me. Actually, there wasn't much to be taken away. God was a mystical source of help when I needed Him, but I never really knew Him and accepted what He has done for me. Now I realize how much He loves me."

I am thankful that woman went through an experience of the absence of the experience of the god she had settled for. She had been found by the true God of creation, Calvary, and Pentecost.

Another old god the true God exposes is the one we have to please by being good enough. Self-justification keeps us from knowing the depth of His grace. The idea is ingrained in our thinking. We feel we are loved and accepted on the basis of our performance. When God seems absent, we think we must have failed to earn His blessing. The problem is, we are never sure we've done enough. In reality, He rejects our self-effort to win His approval. Out of love, He pulls back momentarily, so that we can see our futile attempts at self-generated efforts to climb to heaven on a ladder of human performance. God absents Himself so that we can rediscover Him as He has revealed Himself in Christ.

When you feel the absence of God in your life, have you fallen back into the old syndrome of loving yourself only if you've measured up? Self-condemnation makes us feel unworthy, and it follows inevitably that we can't imagine God loves us. He seems absent, but we have simply projected our attitudes toward ourselves onto Him.

We do the same thing in human relationships. We find it difficult to believe that we are loved in spite of what we do and say; then we imagine people having the same attitudes toward us as we have toward ourselves. The projection becomes so real that we actually believe our feelings toward ourselves are those others have about us. So we blame them for not loving us enough!

We experience a healing moment when someone rejects that idea and says, "Hey, you may be down on yourself, but don't put your feelings into my heart, or your negativism about yourself into my words. I don't happen to be as upset with you as you are with yourself. Give us both a break! I'm for you, on your side, and want what's best for you. Don't make me an enemy when I'm not. You need me too much for that!"

In a much more profound way, that's what the Lord is trying to tell us. Believing so can transform our attitudes toward ourselves and life. Next time we feel God has absented Himself or turned His back on us, let's consider the possibility that we may be making Him an enemy because of our own enmity toward the struggling person inside our own skins.

God is so much more than a super-ego, the enlargement of our condemnatory conscience. He loves us unreservedly, and that truth alone can give us the motive and the courage to change attitudes, patterns, and habits that we condemn so severely in ourselves.

The Start of Something More

Last, the feeling of the absence of God often occurs when we are on the creative edge of wanting Him for who He is and not just for what He can give us.

Often, for example, prayer is little more than a "gimme" game. A tragic secondariness develops. We want the blessings of God without a consistent, transforming relationship with Him. Lovingly, He pulls back from that. He withholds what we ask for until we want the Giver more than the gift.

He allows the terrible feeling of loneliness in our souls for Him until we can say, "Lord, forgive me. I've made You like my impersonal computer. I feed in the data of my needs and expect You to flash up the answer on the screen of my life, but I switch You off as I do my computer when I have what I think I need. Lord, You are the real answer I need. My soul is empty without You. Come, make Your home in me!"

One of the most exciting things I see happening in the church in America today is traditional church people recognizing their need to be filled with the Holy Spirit. The realization often comes in some crisis—a broken relationship, failure, or just a growing dissatisfaction with dull, bland religion. Then people come to grips with how impotent they are to live abundantly, love courageously, forgive unselfishly, or serve joyfully.

The Lord graciously creates a shocking realization of the ruts of routine in which our wheels are stuck. He gives us the gift of an immense dissatisfaction with the frail facsimile of life we've settled for. The feeling is one of His absence, when actually, He's never been closer. At that point of humbling, we are ready to receive repeated infillings of His Spirit for the opportunities and challenges we face.

One of the greatest blessings God can give is to use the feeling of

His absence to make us want Him more than anything He can give us or do for us.

Annie Johnson Flint put that truth in a beautiful way, to express the deepest longing of her heart. In a time of prolonged sickness, she often felt God was absent until she realized that more than healing, she needed Him. A much more profound healing resulted in her soul. When God seems absent, dare to pray this:

Not for peace, not for power,
Not for joy, and not for light;
Not for truth and not for knowledge,
Not for courage for the fight,
Not for strength to do Thy service,
Not for these my prayer shall be,
Not for any gift or graces
But for Thee, Lord, just for Thee
Make me lonely for Thy presence
Every earthly friend above;
Make me thirst for Thy indwelling,
Make me hungry for Thy love
'Til in full and free surrender
I shall yield my life to Thee.
Only then in full perfection
Canst Thou give Thyself to me.

7

Triumph in Trouble
Psalm 46

Just as surely as Psalm 42 has helped us deal with this feeling of the absence of God, Psalm 46 enables us claim the presence of God to triumph in trouble. The purpose of this chapter is to help us get the best out of our troubles.

Your response to that may be, "Wait a minute, Lloyd, I'm reading this book to get rid of trouble, not to get the best out of it!"

I hear you, but the chances of a trouble-free life are slim. The secret we all need to discover is how to react in troubles, what we can learn from them, and how God helps us in the midst of them.

Jesus did not promise a life devoid of trouble but an untroubled heart. "'Let not your heart be troubled,'" He challenged (John 14:1). An untroubled heart can triumph over troubles based on three firm convictions: The Lord is on our side, by our side, and gives us peace inside.

The Psalm of Triumph

This is the triumphant message of the forty-sixth psalm. The psalm eloquently expresses all three convictions. The encouraging progression of the psalmist's witness of how the Lord helped him and Israel to triumph over trouble was occasioned by a radical intervention of the Lord. Many biblical scholars agree that this psalm was written after the Lord stepped in to save Jerusalem from Sennacherib's siege. The historical background helps us to appreciate how the Lord intervenes in our troubles, on time and in time. It shows us again the sublime adequacy of the Lord in the midst of trouble.

Hezekiah was king over Judah. The prophet Micah was used by God to help the king know and trust Him. As a result the monarch brought much needed reform, reestablished the Passover, reopened the temple for worship, and recalled the people to faithfulness and obedience to God.

The Northern Kingdom had already fallen to Sennacherib, the Assyrian conqueror. Now he was on his way to Egypt, conquering and capturing cities and territories in his path. The little kingdom of Judah stood in his way. In the year 701 B.C. the fearsome general raped the small city of Lachish. Then he sent a message to Hezekiah saying, "That's exactly what I'm going to do to Jerusalem."

Talk about trouble! Hezekiah had his, but what he did with Sennacherib's troublesome warning gives us the first key as to what to do when trouble hits us. Hezekiah took the letter and spread it out before the Lord in the temple. Isaiah came to him and warned him not to enter into any alliance to save Jerusalem but to trust in the Lord only. That's exactly what he did, but not without his trust being sorely tested.

The Assyrians advanced to Jerusalem as Sennacherib had warned. They camped around the city walls and prepared to attack the city. The battle was set to begin at midnight. Everyone in Jerusalem waited, gripped by fear.

Then it happened. A mysterious plague swept over the Assyrians and one hundred eighty thousand of them died. At five minutes before twelve, those who were still alive retreated. Sennacherib returned to Nineveh beaten, not by combat with Judah's armies or the strong walls of Jerusalem, but by the Lord's intervention. The holy city was saved.

After the siege was over, the psalmist sang a song of uncontainable praise. It is preserved for us in this forty-sixth psalm of triumph over trouble. In that context we can appreciate all the more fully the message of the psalm and what it can mean to us before, during, and after a siege of trouble in our lives.

On Our Side

God is on our side. That is the meaning of these familiar, oft-repeated words, "God is our refuge and strength, a very present help in trouble" (v. 1). The Hebrew means a "high tower or protection place." The Lord is one to whom we can retreat for refuge and from whom we receive strength in trouble. Just as Hezekiah spread out before the Lord the threats of Sennacherib, so too the first thing to do when trouble strikes is to pray.

During the Civil War Abraham Lincoln cautioned that being on the Lord's side is more important than arrogantly assuming He's on our side. Prayer enables us to see the issues of our trouble and seek the Lord's guidance. The reason for this is that lots of our troubles are caused by ourselves. We may need to seek forgiveness before the Lord can help us. That step is a crucial part of getting the best out of the troubles that disturb us.

Other troubles are caused by other people, and we need to ask the Lord for His guidance in how to solve the trouble by helping the people involved. Usually all trouble has some troubled person causing it. Often the Lord uses the trouble to get to us so that He can get through us to the people involved.

When we ask Him for His perspective and power and are willing to follow orders, He shows us how to communicate His love and forgiveness. He can be counted on to be on our side in that effort! He loves people as much as we are at times disturbed by them. When we pray, honestly seeking what He wants, He gives us the vision of how we are to act and what we are to say. Added to that, He prepares the way before us, opening doors of opportunity. Then He helps us to know His timing. That's crucial. To act precipitously is disastrous; to procrastinate beyond the Lord's appointment is to miss the best opportunity.

How can we know all this? By finding in the Lord both refuge and strength. Retreating from the trouble into communion with Him provides the wisdom, insight, and courage we need to know what to do and when to do it. Often, like Hezekiah, there is little we can do except trust that the Lord will intervene to help us when we face impossible, insurmountable odds.

The psalmist's description of the Lord as "a present help in trouble" in Hebrew means "One willing to be found." Isaiah 55:6 expresses this, "Seek the LORD while He may be found,/Call upon Him while He is near."

The desire to seek the Lord is the direct result of the fact that He has found us and calls us to belong to Him so that we can be free to call upon Him. Surely that's the reason Martin Luther, besieged with trouble, would often say to his friend Philipp Melanchthon, "Come, Philipp, let us sing the forty-sixth psalm." His great hymn, "A Mighty Fortress," is based on this psalm, which expresses our deepest need when there seems to be no way through or out of trouble.

By Our Side

That's when we need the psalmist's next thought. He moved from declaring that God is both a retreat from trouble to strength in the midst of it, to pressing us to face the adequacy of God for whatever happens.

> Therefore we will not fear,
> Though the earth be removed,
> And though the mountains be carried
>   into the midst of the sea;
> Though its waters roar and be troubled,
> Though the mountains shake with its swelling (vv. 2–3).

We are forced to consider the worst that might happen in the trouble we confront, and to ask, "Could that destroy my relationship with the Lord or my assurance that I am alive forever?" We can't live without fear until we know that nothing—what people do or say, the disappointing reversals of life, physical sickness or pain, not even death—can ultimately hurt us or destroy our relationship with the Lord and His promise that we will live with Him forever. Do you have that confidence?

That fearlessness comes not only from knowing God is on our side, but also that He is by our side. That is the meaning of what the psalmist goes on to say in verses 4–7:

> There is a river whose streams shall
>   make glad the city of God,
> The holy place of the tabernacle of the Most High.
> God is in the midst of her, she shall not be moved;
> God shall help her, just at the break of dawn.
> The nations raged, the kingdoms were moved;
> He uttered His voice, the earth melted.
> The LORD of hosts is with us;
> The God of Jacob is our refuge.

These words are rich imagery—metaphors filled with meaning for us. The river is symbolic of the presence of God. We talked about that in our first chapter on the first psalm. The Holy Spirit of the Lord is with us to sustain us. We are never alone. Hezekiah and all of Jerusalem discovered that. The historical reference to the nations raging and falling depict the ravages of the Assyrian conquest, but because Judah trusted in the Lord, His timely intervention of the plague was performed.

When we know that God is by our side, we can confidently expect Him to intervene and do what we most need in our trouble. He is constantly at work preparing people, arranging circumstances, changing situations to bring a resolution to the trouble we face.

My experience has taught me that the quality He desires from us is expectation. He delights to bless us when we surrender our troubles to Him, trust what He will do, and confidently anticipate how He will utilize the snarled mess we've gotten into.

I have a friend who exclaims, whenever trouble hits, "I can't wait to see what the Lord is going to do with this!" The amazing thing is that his life is filled with surprising interventions from the Lord. He knows he belongs to the Lord, accepts the promise that He will help him, and lives with relaxed joyousness as a result. That's not to imply that he sits around and does nothing. When trouble comes, he asks the Lord for orders for anything he should do, but the untangling of the trouble is usually the result of something the Lord does that he could not do.

The reaffirmation that the Lord is by our side in trouble makes the difference between nerve-jangling anxiety and profound peace. I've found it to be true in my pressured life as pastor of a large church, television communicator, speaker, and writer.

Often people ask, "How do you do all you do?"

My response is, "Pray a lot!" I really mean that. If it were not for the river of the Holy Spirit flowing through me, there would be no creativity or production. Years ago I gave up the illusion that I was meant to be a human reservoir of knowledge, insight, wisdom, love, and power. The secret I discovered was that there is no limit to what the Lord's Spirit can do through us if we constantly give Him the glory.

When trouble comes in my family, at work, or in projects the Lord has assigned to me, I am able to make it only if I repeat the words, "The Lord is in this; He will show me what to do, and when I've done all He's guided, He will step in to pull off a miracle in a way I could never have planned." In this past week alone, I've faced six seemingly insolvable sets of trouble. Now at the end of the week as I write this chapter, I am aware that all six have been resolved. The Lord did it!

Not one day of my life goes by without my having to be brought back to the firm conviction that the Lord is by my side. I remind myself of that liberating fact when I get up, when I face problems, when I run out of physical strength or mental creativity, when I become impatient with people, when I speak and write, when I get into troublesome no-win conflicts with people, or when my heart aches over the trouble loved ones endure.

The Lord is by my side.

Say it in your own heart. Emphasize each of the three parts as you repeat it for your trouble right now. *The Lord* is by my side. The Lord *is* by my side. The Lord is by *my side.*

His Peace Inside

Now we can move on to the greatest gift the Lord gives us in order to triumph in trouble. He is not only on our side and by our side, but He gives us peace inside.

The psalmist reviewed the awesome way the Lord intervened for Judah in the siege of Jerusalem. But beholding what God had done was not an occasion for gleeful celebration over the death of one hundred and eighty thousand enemy soldiers—however unrighteous their destructive cause of world dominance. Instead, the Lord told the psalmist, "Be still, and know that I am God."

The progression of the thought is startling. Look at it.

> Come, behold the works of the LORD,
> Who has made desolations in the earth.
> He makes wars cease to the end of the earth;
> He breaks the bow and cuts the spear in two;
> He burns the chariot in the fire (vv. 8–9).

Then suddenly God speaks and our souls tremble.

> Be still, and know that I am God;
> I will be exalted among the nations;
> I will be exalted in the earth! (v. 10).

What does that mean for our triumph in trouble? Magnificently this: what the Lord does for us by intervening to extricate us from

89

seemingly insolvable trouble is to excavate a greater place in our hearts for His indwelling Spirit. He wants to have our awe over what He has done presently to produce adoration for what He will do in the future. When the Lord helps us triumph in trouble, He does not want us to glory in the triumph but in Him.

So often we think we should do something to express our gratitude when He has blessed us in our trouble. Not so. He wants us to absorb the wonder of it all in stillness. Being still and knowing Him as our all-sufficient Lord forms an inseparable cycle: When we are still, we know He is God, and knowing that produces greater stillness. The river of the Spirit now flows in us. A peace pervades us that no future trouble can unsettle or destroy.

Samuel Rutherford once said, "Fool that I was not to know that the messages of God are not to be read through the envelope in which they are enclosed." How God solves our trouble is only the envelope. Look inside. The message is: "Be still, and know that I am God."

Now you can see why I said earlier that the purpose of our study of this psalm was to get the best out of trouble. The Lord's indwelling Spirit and a pervading peace are the best we can discover from seeing what the Lord does with our troubles when we trust Him. We are given a gift no trouble-free life could ever receive. Peace is the result of knowing that we have adequate resources to face anything. If we discover that from the trouble we go through, we can be still in whatever happens to trouble us in the future.

8

Lord, Get Me Out of This!
Psalm 55

What is it that brings the psalmist to say, "'Oh, that I had wings like a dove!/For then I would fly away and be at rest'" (Ps. 55:6). We've all had that feeling! Perhaps you feel it right now—the desire to escape, the longing to be extricated from some painful difficulty or relationship, the urgency to somehow be lifted out of a problem that seems insolvable. But when life flashes a "No Exit" sign, what can we do? We long to get away; yet God calls us back.

The psalmist knew that feeling of having no escape, but so have great people down through the ages. Nathaniel Hawthorne said in the midst of the Civil War, "Lord, it is too present with me, too persistent, too painful. I want out of this." Elizabeth Akers Allen wrote,

> Backward, turn backward
>   O tide of the years,
> I am weary of toil and of tears.
> Toil without recompense,
>   tears all in vain,
> Take them and give me my childhood again.

Even the apostle Paul wanted to get out. When he was imprisoned in Rome, he expressed his desire to "depart and be with Christ" (Phil. 1:23). He didn't receive his request. That was during his first imprisonment in Rome, to be followed by several years of ministry and then a second imprisonment, and finally his execution. Even the Master, Christ, our Lord prayed, "'Father, if it is

Your will, remove this cup from Me; nevertheless not My will, but Yours, be done'" (Luke 22:42).

What is it that causes this feeling of wanting to escape? Some of us simply have become fatigued from the pressures of life, and we truly need to get away and rest. Jesus said to his disciples, ". . . 'Come aside by yourselves to a deserted place and rest a while'. . ." (Mark 6:31). Life has its interludes of rest, its ebb and flow, in which the Lord equips us for the battle. But longing for rest all the time may keep us from the battle for which we were born.

Some others of us say, "Well, I'm hurt. Nobody understands me. I want to get away from it all!" Still others believe that, by leaving, they can make a statement to awaken others to the circumstances that they have been enduring. Others admit defeatedly, "I just don't have what it takes. God, get me out of this!"

A *Psalm of Honesty*

One amazing discovery we make when we read the fifty-fifth psalm is how honest the psalmist was.

> Give ear to my prayer, O God,
> And do not hide Yourself from my supplication.
> Attend to me, and hear me;
> I am restless in my complaint, and moan noisily,
> Because of the voice of the enemy,
> Because of the oppression of the wicked;
> For they bring down trouble upon me,
> And in wrath they hate me.
> My heart is severely pained within me,
> And the terrors of death have fallen upon me.
> Fearfulness and trembling have come upon me,
> And horror has overwhelmed me (vv. 1–5).

Those words may sound like an exaggerated description of the difficulties of life. We may not feel that strongly, but we do empathize with what follows:

And I said, "Oh, that I had wings like a dove!
For then I would fly away and be at rest.
Indeed, I would wander far off,
    And remain in the wilderness" (vv. 6–7).

Jeremiah expressed the same longing. "Oh, that I had in the wilderness/A lodging place for wayfaring men;/That I might leave my people . . ." (9:2). What do you do when you feel like that?

Three Things "Escape Artists" Need to Know

There are times when we have caused the reason for our wanting to escape. Other times it is caused by difficult people. I know husbands and wives who blame each other and long for a way out of their marriage. I talk to people who are in jobs they no longer find rewarding and are looking for fulfillment in some other job.

There are those who wish they could pare down their list of friends and drop some of those who are a constant burden. And what about the people we have trusted who let us down when we needed them the most? Do you know anyone you want to get off your back? We all want to get away from people and life's demands at times.

1. Be sure you know what you mean by *rest*. "If I had the wings of a dove, I would fly away and rest," says the psalmist. What is rest? In the context of the Scriptures, rest is not geography but a condition of the soul. Rest is a relationship with the Lord—His peace indwelling us. If you can't have that quality of peace in the battle, you can't have it at all!

Of course, there are necessary times of vacation rest. Visiting the mountains is refreshing. They are wonderful to ski upon and hike over. I enjoy lakes to fish in and renew my strength. Many like desert places to warm their bodies as well as their souls. Beautiful country places can give us hope and encouragement. Yet, we're not born for these. We were born for the battle.

2. When we want to "get away from it all," we need to remember that wherever we go, we'll bring our greatest problem with
us.

On a recent flight across the country, I was seated next to a
woman who seemed very troubled. During the meal we struck up a
conversation. When she learned I was a pastor she began to pour
out her woes. Her husband, children, and friends had not lived up
to her high expectations. She was even less satisfied with herself.
She told me that she was on her way to an "escape vacation."

I tried to build on that and encouraged her to use the time alone
to rediscover God's love for her.

"But I'm not going to be alone," she said. "I've got my worst
enemy with me."

I looked around, wondering where this person was seated on the
plane. I saw a few I thought would qualify. Then she said, "This
person goes with me everywhere!"

"Who is it?" I asked.

"I," she said.

I told her that was admirable honesty, but then went on to talk
about how to make herself her best friend.

We see those beautiful travel posters . . . "Get away from it all,"
they invite us enticingly. Often I want to go into the travel agency
and take a great big pen and write, "There's something you can't get
away from—yourself."

3. Define for yourself a reason great enough to stay in the battle.
One of the major things a crisis does to a nation is that it draws the
people into a cause greater than any of us. I often ask people around
the world, "What's the most exciting time of your life?"

So often they remember the time of World War II. They say, "At
least we had something to fight for that was bigger than us." I talk to
people in London about that and they say, "Oh, those were exciting
times. Terrible, but exciting. At least we had something to fight for
that was worthy of the battle."

Do you have such a reason to stay in the battle that's greater than you, greater than your comfort, greater than your satisfaction, greater than your desire?

The Exit Syndrome

As a man explained about his marriage, "I got tired of living with my first wife. There was more trouble than I could ever imagine in a marriage, so I got married to another woman. Well, she was as bad as the first one." I suspect he'll have the same difficulty with the third, unless he stops running from the problem person who lives inside his own skin!

People are peripatetic when it comes to their churches. Often they stay with a congregation only as long as it satisfies them and doesn't disturb them too much. I went to a conference recently where I talked to three couples about their church. I was interested to discover that two of those couples had left their church and one had stayed. As I analyzed all three couples, however, I was disturbed to see that in reality none of them had stayed emotionally, even the one that was still there. That couple was so filled with criticism and negativism that they would not have been satisfied with anything the pastor said or proposed. Their commitment to Christ had not grown into faithfulness to His body, the church. Until there is a conversion transformation in them, followed by an infilling of His Spirit of both love and acceptance, they will not be happy in any congregation.

The same problem exists for many people in their work. "What can you do for me?" so many say to a personnel manager when they apply for a job. "What are the compensations?" "Tell me about the time off." "Do you follow all the laws to be sure that I'm protected here?"

Whatever happened to the rawboned spirit of commitment that believes God is Lord and we've been called not to be comforted but to minister; the kind of spirit where we get to work instead of asking everyone to work for us? Whatever happened to loyalty? Things get a little tough and we say, "If I had the wings of a dove, I'd fly away." The problem is that some have flown away; but the tragedy is, they are AWOL without ever having left camp.

A man came to see me about his marriage. He was involved with another woman. He said, "I've met somebody who can't keep her hands off me, and I'm married to a woman who has no time for me."

His Christian wife had tuned him out even though she dutifully continued washing his socks and cooking his food. Neither the man nor his wife was blameless. Both had acted out their inner desire to escape the responsibility of offering initiating love as the first step back to communication and the hard work of meeting each other's needs.

I could fill an entire book with examples of people suffering from the spiritual virus of escapism. Eventually we discover that there is another person in addition to ourselves from whom we cannot escape: The Lord! The rest of Psalm 55 attests to that.

The Point of Change

Notice the magnificent thing that happened to the psalmist. Once he confessed the fact that he wanted to fly away, be at rest, and he poured out all his anger and frustration, he found his deepest need was for the Lord. After his venom was emptied, his mood suddenly changed. He said to himself and to the congregation of Israel, "Cast your burden on the LORD,/And He shall sustain you;/ He shall never permit the righteous to be moved" (v. 22). When our trust is ultimately in Him, and we dare to live out His will in the crises of life, He will give us what we need.

There is a great difference between "the wings of a dove to fly away" and "the wings of an eagle" that give the power to soar until we get perspective. The eagle can fly with mighty strength, but it does not fly away. Its power comes from the jet stream.

> . . . those who wait on the LORD
> Shall renew their strength;
> They shall mount up with wings like eagles,
> They shall run and not be weary,
> They shall walk and not faint (Is. 40:31).

The point is clear. The Lord wants to give us the raw courage to face life as it is and receive power to change it, beginning with ourselves. Don't leave the battle. Your post of duty was elected for you, and there you will find more of God than you'll find in a self-imposed exile of escape. He's there in the battle with you!

Returning to the Front

There's a wonderful poem that talks about the difference between the towns of responsibility and the fields of comfort and ease. I'd like you to put in for the word *town* whatever is the battleground for you.

> I said, "Let me walk in the fields."
>   He said, "No; walk in the town."
> I said, "There are no flowers there."
>   He said, "No flowers, but a crown."
> I said, "But the skies are black,
>   There is nothing but noise and din;"
> And He wept as He sent me back;
>   "There is more," He said, "there is sin."
> I said, "But the air is thick
>   and the fogs are veiling the sun."
> He answered, "Yet, souls are sick,
>   and souls in the dark undone."
> I said, "I shall miss the light,
>   and friends will miss me, they say."
> He answered, "Choose tonight
>   if I am to miss you, or they.

I pleaded for time to be given.
   He said, Is it hard to decide?
It will not seem hard in heaven
   to have followed your Guide."
I cast one look at the fields,
   then set my face to the town;
He said, "My child, do you yield?
   Will you leave the flowers for the crown?"
Then into His hand went mine;
   And into my heart came He;
And I walk in the light divine,
The path I had feared to see.[1]

Dare to leave the field and the flowers of ease, and get back into the battle. The Lord will bless you. Cast your burden on Him and He will renew your strength. He will sustain you. He will never permit the righteous to be moved.

9

How to Receive Power
Psalm 62

Some years ago, I got lost while backpacking in the wilderness in
northern Canada. I went in circles for hours trying to find the logging road and the way back to where my friends were camped.

Finally, I came to a narrow path overgrown with brush. I followed it until it came to a fork in the path. Staked out on one of the
two alternative paths ahead was a rough-hewn sign. On it a trapper,
well known in that territory, had written instructions in bold letters.
"This is the *only* way out!" The trapper's name was printed out at
the bottom.

As I took his commanding instruction, I thought about the authority expressed in that word *only*. I had to admit that I didn't like
to be told that there was only one way to go. A real temptation
surged up within me to take the opposite path. But noticing that the
sun was setting, I knew I had no choice. I took the trapper's "only"
way and found my way to the logging road and back to camp just
before dark.

None of us likes to be told that there is only one way to go any-
where or do anything. The mere suggestion that there is no other
way makes us want to disprove the claim by finding another way.
That spirit can be very creative in discovering new truth in scientific
research or in superseding the tried but not altogether true ways
people have established. The adventuresome spirit that says,
"There must be a better way of doing this," has blazed the trail for
progress. Some of us have to try out what others assert is the "only"
way before we can be sure for ourselves. Then, when we find there

is no other way, the assertions of others become our own assurance.

That's what happened to the psalmist. He had been raised with the truth that God only was the source of power for salvation, security, and strength. Then he went through an experience that made the conviction of others the rock foundation of his life. The incident happened when he was under debilitating attack and criticism by his enemies. He had to defend his faith.

In marshaling all he believed and comparing it with what his opponents believed, he was more sure than ever. He was forced to see the immense difference between trusting in God's power and nothing else and a vague cultural religion that depended on wealth, position, and human power.

At the conclusion of his meditation recorded for us in Psalm 62 he arrived at a firm conviction for himself, ". . . That power belongs to God" (v. 11). That conclusion didn't come quickly or easily, but it was the result of all that God meant to him and how little He meant to his adversaries.

God "Only" or God "And"?

We are thankful the psalmist went through what he did. Because of it we are recipients of one of the clearest statements of faith in God's power in the psalter. He tried and tested the "Only Way Out!" signpost of his historic faith and found it to be reliable and true. Then he could say about his God, "He only is my rock and my salvation" (v. 2).

In the confession of his reaffirmed faith, he used the Hebrew word *'ak* four times. Look carefully at this. The word is used here in two ways: as an assertive, *truly*; and with a restrictive force, *only*. (1) "*Truly* my soul silently waits for God" (v. 1); (2) "He *only* is my rock and my salvation" (v. 2); (3) "My soul, wait silently for God *alone*" (v. 5); and again, (4) "He *only* is my rock and salvation; He is my defense" (v. 6).

The psalmist also used the word to describe the singleminded determination of his antagonists and to contrast their negative purpose with his own positive experience of God's power: "They *only* consult to cast him [a man] down from his high position" (v. 4).

The implication is that both the psalmist and his enemies were Israelites who believed in God. However, the vital faith of the psalmist led him to trust only in God; his enemies' vacillating faith had added secondary loyalties that motivated their only passion—the desire to pull down anyone who rose higher or had more than they. The difference between the psalmist and his antagonists was the immense differential between "God only" and "God and."

As I studied this psalm and realized my own need for greater power, I saw the inseparable relationship between receiving God's power and saying, "He only is my rock and salvation." Could I say that potent word *only* and mean it? What about lesser securities of position, prestige, prosperity? Could I do without them and trust only in God for power? What about you?

The more I thought about that the more a deep conviction formed in my mind. Then it was ordered into a concise sentence I believe God worded in my thought processes as a basis of an exposition of this psalm. I wrote it down exactly as it was given to me: "Those who trust in God only, have Him and everything else; those who trust in Him and anything else, end up without Him and nothing else."

Demanding, impelling, liberating? Yes, all three. The truth is a blast through the restrictive barrier that holds us back from soaring in the flow of supernatural power. Here is greatness as we all were meant to experience it. Then we can say with the psalmist,

God has spoken once,
Twice I have heard this:
That power belongs to God.
Also to You, O Lord, belongs mercy;
For You render to each one according to his work (vv. 11–12).

Belief: Not Always Pain Free

The key words are *work, mercy,* and *power.* What work can we do? On this side of Calvary, an empty tomb, and Pentecost, our work is vividly defined by Jesus, ". . . 'This is the work of God, that you believe in Him whom He sent'" (John 6:29). In accepting that fact we experience true mercy and unmerited and unqualified love; and when we trust in those words as our only hope, we receive unlimited power.

To realize that wholehearted, abandoned trust, *we may have to pass through what the psalmist experienced.* In the first two verses he expressed his inherited faith that God only was his rock, salvation, and defense. In verses 3 and 4 he compared his faith with that of his adversaries. From that exercise he emerged stronger than ever with a personal faith. The belief of Israel had become his own.

He reiterated what he had said from rote memory in verses 1 and 2, but now he was sure for himself. In his earlier declaration he said that because of God he would not be greatly moved. In his refined faith, after the fires of conflict, he simply said, "I shall not be moved."

The difference is immense in my mind—the difference between saying, "I will not be moved very much" to "I will not be moved at all!" In the Psalms, to be moved means to be unsettled, to be thrown off balance, to fall from our confidence, to be defeated in conflict, or to stumble in slippery places. The psalmist found the solid Rock of Ages, and his confidence was only in Him. Such assurance enabled him to say, "Trust in Him at all times, you people;/Pour our your heart before him;/God is a refuge for us" (v. 8).

Reaffirming his trust, he once again looked at the insecurity of those who do not trust in God only. Their life is limited to this brief span of time on earth, they build themselves up and put others down, and they trust in material wealth regardless of how it is acquired (see vv. 9–10). Most of all, human power and prowess is substituted for receiving power from the Lord and depending only on Him. Trusting in His power and in nothing else gives us a flow of supernatural power—and through His power comes other blessings.

We all need power—power to think God's thoughts after Him, power to do His will as He reveals it, power in our bodies to act on what He has shown us to do. The secret the psalmist discovered is now an open secret. The Lord pours out His greatest blessings on those who put their trust only in Him. To accomplish that, He gives us the three things we desperately need. The psalmist defined them as a rock, salvation, and a sure defense.

Think of it this way: God Himself is the rock. His nature is our sure foundation. He gives what He is—love—the source of His power, of His forgiveness of our sins, and of the strength He gives us to live daily in obedience to Him He is the Intervenor when we are in trouble; the One who opens doors of opportunity for the next step of His strategy for us; the source of strength when we are ill. He gives us His comfort when we grieve; courage when we are tempted to give up; and companionship when we walk through the valley of the shadow of death. Who else can provide that quality of power? God only!

Three Recipients

Three stories of three different people who found that God only was their only rock and salvation exemplify what I've been trying to say.

The first was a man who came to me seeking to know God personally. He had been a nonmember participant in my congregation. He had watched our worship, listened to the sermons, watched the joyous countenances on the faces of the people. He said, "Lloyd, I want to know Christ. I want to have what you and these people have. What can I do to qualify?"

And I said, "Nothing."

Astounded, he said, "What?"

I reiterated, "Nothing. There is absolutely nothing that you can do to qualify, but there is something you can receive that will enable you to appropriate the love, forgiveness, and power that God offers to you."

"What is that? What is the gift?" he asked.

"The gift is faith. Recognizing what God has done for you in Christ at the cross brings forth the power of faith."

I took him back into the heart of God, described to him the blessed faithfulness of God, told him that he was loved and forgiven and accepted. Then I saw a radiance begin to shine on his face. And he said, "I believe. I believe that Christ died for me."

That was the beginning. He could say, "God only is my salvation." Not his self-justification, not his good works, not his adequacy, not what he was or what he had achieved, but only God could give him the power to believe and grasp the Cross. He could say with the hymn, "Nothing in my hand I bring, simply to thy Cross I cling." He had discovered the only way.

Paul put it clearly, "'Nor is there salvation in any other, for there is no other name under heaven given among men by which we must be saved'" (Acts 4:12). The same power we witness in Christ in His ministry is available to us through His indwelling Spirit. Spiritual power is received from no one else. From within us, He enables us to know His mind, have His power to know what He is guiding us to do, and receive His enabling strength to dare to attempt it.

The psalm challenges us to "Pour out your heart before Him" (v. 8). We empty ourselves of our requests, needs, and will to control. Into our empty hearts, He comes to abide with power.

The second story is of a woman. She was my last appointment after a long afternoon of counseling people in need. I began with, "How are you?"

"Not very well," she answered.

"What's the trouble?"

She said, "If I can only make it through this crisis, if I can only have what it takes to make it. . ."

I said, "Dear friend, you don't need to have what it takes to make it. You can say 'God only is my salvation, my deliverance, my hope, my strength for this crisis,' and you'll come through this acknowledging that He saw you through it. But you must trust Him unreservedly. Can you do that?"

We talked about the specific crisis that was before her and then we prayed, spreading her problem out before the Lord and giving her needs totally over to Him. He stepped in and gave her exactly what she needed. His power was released in wisdom, courage, and greater forgiving love than she possessed.

Later she said, "Only God alone, only God could have helped me, and He gave me the power to make it."

The last story is of a man facing his death. He came to me and he said, "Lloyd, I've got three months to live. Will you help me to know how to die?"

We talked in depth about dying and then he said, "But how can I qualify for heaven? What can I do to be sure that when I walk through the valley of the shadow of death I will only be at the beginning of my eternal life?"

As with the first man, I said, "Nothing."

"There must be something I can do to be sure."

"Only one thing. Accept the salvation purchased for you by Jesus Christ at Calvary. Then if there are things that you need to straighten out, restitutions you need to make, reconciliations to be accomplished, go do it in these three months. But know this, that when you meet your Savior, it will be with nail pierced hands that He reaches out for you, and it will be to a pierced side that He draws you, and it will be His blood that cleanses you."

In a deep time of prayer, he said, "The Lord only is my salvation. I am afraid of dying no more. Thank You, Lord, for the power to die glorifying You!"

Can you say that with surety?

In the end and in everything before we get there we say,

Grace taught my soul to pray
Grace made my eyes overflow
'Tis grace has kept me to this day,
And will not let me go.[1]

When I completed my study of Psalm 62, I read over again the sentence the Lord had given me. Then I reworded it using personal pronouns. It became a reaffirmation of my trust in God only: "When I put my trust in God only, I have Him and everything else, when I trust in Him plus anything else, I end up without Him and have nothing else."

The one who is your only Rock, Salvation, and Sure Defense may be urging you to make that affirmation of faith your own. I believe you will find it the secret of power. I have. It's the only way out!

10

Confusing Comparisons
Psalm 73

I saw a bumper sticker which both amazed and alarmed me. In bold, black letters it said, "Prosperity: Your Divine Right!" It was displayed on the bumper of a big, new luxury car.

That started me thinking. Is prosperity my divine right? Do I have *any* rights before God? I took it that the word *right* was being used to imply something to which one has just or lawful claim. Then I thought about what it means to be right with God through the atonement of Jesus Christ. That doesn't always mean material prosperity.

The Arrogance of Demanding Rights

Always is an almighty word. Using it, or even implying it, is dangerous when we are talking about the way God deals with us. He is marvelously original in the ways He expresses His providence. To say that prosperity is the only way He blesses would be wrong. I know too many people who have found God when their false god of prosperity toppled, and I also know many who have fallen into the trap of materialism and no longer put God first in their lives.

Try out that bumper sticker saying on Jeremiah, Isaiah, Job, or Jesus! They'd tell you that those words are sophomorically simplistic and don't cover the truth of the total sweep of revelation in Scripture.

In portions of the Old Testament, the people of Israel equated material prosperity with God's blessing. That's implied in one stage of the evolving understanding of salvation. A man's land, the size of his herds, the fruition of his family measured the extent of God's care.

But don't stop there. Deal with God's judgment on Israel when prosperity became a substitute for faithfulness and obedience. Read the prophets and listen to the wisdom writers. They discovered that God was gracious in what He gave and what He withheld. The heresy that prosperity is always our divine right bypasses the obvious development through Scripture.

All that's said about God's dealing with us must be brought under the bright light of the Lord Jesus Christ. He confronted the Pharisees, who believed they had rights before God. He also taught that we are to seek first God's kingdom and His righteousness. Material things are not the measure of the person. When Jesus said that all things would be added to us following the obedience of seeking first God's kingdom, He did not mean that those things were our right. Rather, they are an expression of His love for us.

In fact, Jesus put such a low priority on riches that He said that it was more difficult for a rich man to enter the kingdom of God than for a camel to go through the eye of a needle. What I think He meant was that when we think our riches are our right, they stand in the way of realizing either an abundant spiritual life or an eternal life with the Lord.

The Problems with Prosperity

What do we do if we believe prosperity is our divine right and our prosperity is reversed? Or what if we hold firmly to the belief that God heals all physical ailments on our timing and in the way we've asked, and we don't get a ready response to the orders we've sent to God in our prayers? Can God use the reversals in our finances? Can He use the period of patient waiting for healing as well as the actual healing of our diseases?

We must avoid the idea that God sends difficulties. He doesn't have to. There are enough to go around in our fallen world. What we can say is that He uses them to bring us into deeper fellowship with Him. We are in dangerous territory when we universalize our own experience or build a whole theology on the ways we've observed God working in the past. He is constantly doing a new thing and contradicts our pet theories that would put Him in our straight-jacket.

I have a further difficulty with the divine right of prosperity. This false teaching contradicts the best of the American ideal and can slow up our progress in correcting social injustice. The forefathers and mothers who pushed back the frontiers and built this nation would have scoffed at the idea that prosperity was their right. They would have quickly affirmed that opportunity is a gift of God. They worked hard as they cooperated with His strength. Most of them were quick to give Him the glory for the privilege of developing the resources at their disposal. The essence of the American spirit is not that prosperity is our right, but that it is our possibility, if combined with dedication to hard work and dependence on God's strength in the use of the talents and resources He has given us.

That prompts a comment on social justice. There are cultural conditions that debilitate people from the full expression of their industriousness. We have struggled too long and hard to bring equal opportunity to all races and both sexes to imply that prosperity, rather than the right to work, is our divine right. Equal rights means the responsibility of our society to give every individual the right to get training, procure a job of his or her choice, and enjoy the fruit of that labor. We can't blame God for the fact that it has taken so long to establish these rights for everyone in the United States. The truth is that we hold back progress ourselves with prejudice and a distortion of the American dream.

But the most disturbing result of the idea that prosperity is our right is that it leads us into an equivocating eddy of envy. We compare our level of prosperity with others. We end up wondering if God loves some more than others. Most of all we demand an explanation of why some who are not as righteous as we seem to get ahead.

A *Psalm of Understanding*

That was exactly the problem the psalmist faced in Psalm 73. We go through the excruciating experience of the long, weary flight of the bird of distorted understanding of blessing, until it comes home to roost! The psalmist lived in a time when the Hebrew people believed that the blessing of the Lord was *always* manifested in material prosperity. Suddenly he faced a time when life fell apart and he said, "Where is my God now?"

He had gotten caught in the syndrome of "belief for blessing." He had believed, and God's blessings weren't coming according to his agenda. He asked the question, "Why? I've kept all the rules. I've followed the Lord. I've kept the law. Why then do evil people, who make no pretense of believing in Him, receive blessings from God?"

Have you ever asked that question? Who hasn't! We try to run our affairs honestly and somebody else who breaks all the rules— cheats and connives and manipulates—has a better bottom line than we have. We say, "God, I trusted You. Why didn't You pull it off better for me?"

I talked to a woman the other day who was having trouble in her marriage. She complained, "It isn't that I covet my neighbor's husband; I covet the relationship that she has with her husband." Recognizing what she was lacking in her own life, she was envious of a neighbor who didn't even believe in God. Yet, the neighbor had a relationship in her marriage she didn't have, and the woman was envious.

We struggle to pay our mortgages and are faithful in paying our bills and living a responsible life. Then we walk into the home of an affluent person who gives no pretense of believing in God and we wonder, "God, what are You doing? I trust You and You didn't give me all this. Here's somebody who doesn't even care about You who is getting ahead."

There's the pitfall. When we think that prosperity is the sure sign that God is blessing us, we'll get into trouble every time because there is always someone who is more prosperous than we. Envy begins to grow in the polluted swamp of that kind of confusing comparison.

Psalm 73 takes us through a wonderful progression. There are three things here I want to underline.

The Futility of Human Comparisons

First of all, we are shown the futility of confusing comparisons. The psalmist needed God, not what the wicked had or what they had achieved without God. He had missed the salient point. In using a *quid pro quo* on God, he had tried to manipulate Him. He had lost the wonder of God's originality. That God had allowed some of the wicked to prosper was really none of his business even though the wicked were getting away with things that he wouldn't even dare do.

Yet note how blatantly the psalmist broke the Tenth Commandment in the process. He thought he kept all of the Commandments. He took pride in the fact that he placed no false god or graven image before the Lord God. But he broke the commandment about coveting. That transgression always happens when we measure God's blessing in terms of what we get and how much we accumulate.

Dante described those in the purgatory of the envious as being "beggars with their eyes sewn shut." Envy is always a hungry beggar, who never has enough. Our eyes register our comparisons of what we have with what others have achieved. Think of what wonders we miss when our roving eyes are focused on the wrong things.

Envy hits all of us at times. It comes when we refuse to accept the unique and special wonder each of us is by God's grace. Envy is really an unstable state of grace, putting our eyes on other people rather than on God. We forget how wondrously He has blessed us in spite of everything, and we are kept from getting to work in the use of the talents and gifts entrusted to us.

A Change in Attitude

The second movement of the psalm shows the only solution for this: confession. The psalmist considered what his attitude had done to him. He had been untrue to the covenant and realized what would happen if all of Israel reacted as he had. He had been tempted to emulate the wicked in order to have what they had. The prosperity of the wicked had gotten to him and had loosened his grip on eternal values. When it got to be too much for him he said,

> When I thought how to understand this,
> It was too painful for me—
> Until I went into the sanctuary of God;
> Then I understood their end (vv. 16–17).

The purpose of our life is to meet and know the living God and to come into an intimate relationship with Him. The years of this life, however long or short they be, are for one purpose—to know Him personally and to spend eternity with Him. The abundant life of fellowship with Him during this life cannot always be measured in the material wealth that we have. God is not against prosperity. He wants to bless us, but we can never demand it or say that He is not blessing us unless we have everything we want, when we want it.

There was a wonderful play on Broadway some years ago called *The Best Man*. In it an ex-president who was dying of cancer was talking to a candidate for the presidency. He asked a penetrating question of one of the young, rising political leaders. "Bill, do you believe in God?"

Bill's response was that he was an Episcopalian.

"That wasn't what I asked," the ex-president retorted. "I'm a Methodist and I'm still asking: Do you believe there is a God and a Day of Judgment and a hereafter?" Then he confessed that he was dying of cancer. He went on, "I tell you, son, I'm scared to death . . . I don't fancy being just a pinch of dust."

The young aspirant to the presidency tried to comfort him with the fact that the ex-president had done so many wonderful things and his influence was going to go on. Facing eternal issues, the ex-president responded, "I suggest you tell yourself that when you have to face a whole pile of nothing up ahead."[1]

That's what the psalmist realized. He saw, perhaps for the first time, that there is ultimate judgment; that the purpose of this life is to know God, and if he didn't come to know Him in this life, he would not live in eternity with Him. Suddenly, the psalmist saw things in perspective and realized that the blessing of God is a relationship with Himself whether or not he received blessings in material wealth. He realized that God deals with different people in different ways.

Finally, the psalmist gave up his assumed right to judge the wicked. Through communion with the Lord in the sanctuary, he saw his envy for what it really was—a need for the assurance of God's love for him. A renewed experience of that truth led to the confession of his own sin:

> Thus my heart was grieved,
> And I was vexed in my mind.
> I was so foolish and ignorant;
> I was like a beast before You (vv. 21–22).

Finally he came to the triumphant conclusion, which was in a comforting conviction that could give him courage to live his days. After he had started his case and surrendered it to God, he could say,

> Nevertheless I am continually with You;
> You hold me by my right hand.

You will guide me with Your counsel,
And afterward receive me to glory.
Whom have I in heaven but You?
And there is none upon earth that I
   desire besides You.
My flesh and my heart fail;
But God is the strength of my heart
   and my portion forever (vv. 23–26).

The Power to Praise

That brings us to the third point this psalm brings to mind. The greatest blessing that God can give is the power to bless Him. That's what the wicked can't do. The psalmist came to the realization that the most magnificent blessing of all was that he was able to entrust his life to God and live confidently, trusting Him and not the material things—or the lack of them—that he had acquired. He dared to live in complete trust.

Do you have such a trust? The danger of the kind of envy the psalmist struggled with is that we spend our energies comparing our fortunes with other people's and never get to the reason we were born.

An old frontier preacher who wasn't very adept in refined ways of leading funerals once pointed over to a casket and said, "I want you to know that this corpse was a member of this church for thirty years." It is possible to be a spiritual corpse and still be alive, but not really alive.

Prosperity is not your divine right, but a relationship with God is. His grace and His mercy, His power and His love—these are your divine right. It was in order to bestow those gifts that He created you. My question is, Have you fulfilled the reason for which you were born, or have you gotten caught up in the whirlwind of envy and missed the Lord Himself?

Joseph Addison penned these truths in a marvelous way:

When all Thy mercies, O my God,
   My rising soul surveys;
Transported with the view I'm lost in
   wonder, love and praise.
Through every period of my life Thy
   goodness I'll pursue,
The desert paths, the glory bright,
   the precious theme renew.
Through all eternity to Thee my joyous
   song I'll raise,
But, O dear God, eternity's far too short
   to utter all Thy praise.[2]

11

Adventuresome Living
Psalm 84

Once we are set free from confusing comparisons of ourselves with others, we are ready to get on with our own unique pilgrimage. Life is a pilgrimage toward the special reason for which each of us was born.

What Is a Pilgrim?

The term *pilgrim* describes who we are and where we are going. The two alternative definitions of a pilgrim illuminate that. The Latin word *pelegrinus* actually means "foreigner" or "one who journeys to foreign lands." The pilgrim is a wayfarer or adventurer in a place that is not his home. Ultimately, that is what we are meant to be. We are never quite at home in any place or condition in this life. The Lord alone is our security and meaning wherever we are. Whenever things or people become more important than our relationship with Him, our hearts become fettered to false gods. Bound only to Him, we are free to press on to do His will.

That leads us to the second definition of a pilgrim. He is one who travels to a shrine or holy place as an act of devotion. For us, that shrine is not in a building or a place hallowed because of a previous revelation of the Lord. Rather the holy place is a life in His presence, under His guidance, and in obedience to His revealed plan for us individually.

This chapter is purposely set between our consideration of freedom from comparisons and the next chapter on eternal security. We have been released from bondage to anyone or anything so that we can know that our eternal destiny is sure in heaven in the heart of God. In between, during the years of this life, we can live the abundant life adventurously as the Lord's pilgrims. For that pilgrimage we need a pilgrim's purpose, a pilgrim's heart, and the pilgrim's power.

All three are magnificently set forth in the eighty-fourth psalm. The psalmist described a pilgrim on his way to Jerusalem. We are not sure whether he was describing a pilgrimage he was about to make or one he remembered fondly. In either case, longing for the presence of the living God is the dominant note. We feel the pulsebeat of a homesick man who can be at home nowhere but in communion with Him.

A *Pilgrim's Purpose*

Verses 1–4 express the pilgrim's purpose:

> How lovely is Your tabernacle,
> O LORD of hosts!
> My soul longs, yes, even faints
> For the courts of the LORD;
> My heart and my flesh cry out for the living God (vv. 1–2).

The psalmist's purpose was also his passion. He used poetic language to describe the tabernacle of the Lord of hosts. *How dear* or *how beloved* expresses his devotion.

The word *tabernacle* in Hebrew is actually plural and expresses love for the various parts of which the temple in Jerusalem was composed. For us, the word expresses the Lord's omnipresence. His tabernacles, or dwelling places, are everywhere for us and His availability is wondrously constant. He invades all of our days and creates a longing in us to know, love, and serve Him. He is the LORD *of hosts* of all His people here and the heavenly hosts. He is revealed to each of us individually and yet, mysteriously, to all who call on Him in every place.

He is *my* God and *our* God in the same instant, and He can be known in an intimate relationship when our soul, heart, and flesh cry out for Him. The *soul* is our spirit, the life breath within us, and the port of entry of the Lord's Spirit in us. Our *heart* in the Hebrew sense is our mind, emotion, and will. Once the Lord calls us into communion with Him, He takes command of our thinking, emotional responses to His love, and the decisions of our wills. The *flesh* is more than the body, and here it denotes our humanness in desperate need of God. The flesh joins with the heart in affirming the soul's longing for the living God. As much as the psalmist yearned to be in the temple in Jerusalem, his true longing was for God Himself. His purpose was to be in His presence, to worship Him, and to order his whole life as an expression of praise.

For the psalmist, being at home with the Lord in the temple was like a sparrow or a swallow finding a nest, a secure place. What that nest meant to the sparrow or swallow, the Lord and His temple meant to the psalmist. Such is the meaning of his adoration:

> Even the sparrow has found a home,
> And the swallow a nest for herself,
> Where she may lay her young—
> Even Your altars, O LORD of hosts,
> My King and my God.
> Blessed are those who dwell in Your house;
> They will still be praising You (vv. 3–4).

What does all that mean to you and me? We are challenged to wonder if the Lord means that quality of purpose for us. We all have a purpose. For some of us it is survival, just making it through today and however many problem-filled tomorrows are dished out to us. For others, life's purpose is security, to be free from worry or fear. The driving passion for others of us is happiness, that nebulous contentment in having everything going our way.

For many, the goal of life is success, the accomplishment of progressive advancement in our work and the monetary payoff which allows us to accumulate the trophies of material prosperity. Still others express their purpose in the people they love, though that love is often dominated by need. These purposes create the fabric of our value systems, as well as our actions and reactions to life. The danger is that we can believe in God and yet be driven by any one of these lesser purposes. None of the above is wrong. The problem is that they are inadequate as the ultimate purpose of our life.

How would you state your purpose? What is the guiding goal of your life? What's the one thing beneath everything else that determines what you do and what you think is important? What is it that sets your priorities? What controls how you react to life's challenges and opportunities? On what basis do you decide to do one thing and not another?

Our temptation is to respond with religious jargon that is not supportable by our actions and attitudes. Honestly writing out our statement of purpose can be a very liberating experience. Then we have a chance to discern whether our purpose is God's purpose for us. How do we know that? He told us plainly in Christ. We must put Him first in our lives, accept His love and forgiveness, be filled with His Spirit, and live a supernatural life as a riverbed of the flow of His power. He has called us to abide in Him and, as an act of will, to invite Him to abide in us.

I like the way the Scots Shorter Catechism puts our true purpose in the first question and answer. "What is man's chief end? To glorify God and enjoy Him forever." That succinct statement has stood the test of time as a benchmark for everything we do and say, our relationships and responsibilities, our work and money, and our hopes and plans for the future.

No one has ever been sandbagged by guilt into a grand purpose like that. We gain such a perspective from being loved by the One we seek to glorify and enjoy. Lesser purposes are simply an expression of an inadequate experience of grace. Once we have known the Lord's unqualified love and felt the power of His presence, we are given an unquenchable thirst to know more of Him and grow into a deeper relationship with Him in both prayer and faithfulness in all we do. That's what the psalmist expressed. His longing for God was because He had known the joy of the presence of the living God.

The Pilgrim's Heart

Why this emphasis on the pilgrim's purpose? The right purpose gives birth to a pilgrim's heart that will take problems in stride with optimism and courage. The reason we need a purpose as great as the psalmist's is so we can develop a positive attitude to the challenges along the way to the accomplishment of that purpose. The psalmist progressed to that viable hopefulness in difficulty in the flow of his thought in verses 5–7:

> Blessed is the man whose strength is in You,
> Whose heart is set on pilgrimage.
> As they pass through the Valley of Baca,
> They make it a spring;
> The rain also covers it with pools.
> They go from strength to strength;
> Every one of them appears before God in Zion.

We need to dig out the deeper meaning of what these words mean. The pilgrims on the way to Jerusalem had to pass through an arid, foreboding, grim passageway called the Valley of Baca. The word *bācā'* refers to balsam trees or aspens and is used to indicate a tree or shrub that grows in arid places. Thus, the New English Bible translates the Valley of Baca as "the thirsty valley." The psalmist may have been referring to Rephaim, the only place referred to in the Old Testament as a valley of trees like that (see 2 Sam. 5:22–23).

The important information for our exposition is that the psalmist wanted to establish that the way to Jerusalem had to be made through a difficult, dry valley that offered no water for tired and thirsty travelers. All there was on first observation were scrawny balsam trees, craggy rocks, and no water. The Valley of Baca became metaphorical for the problems that had to be endured to get on to Jerusalem. For us, the implication is of all the difficult, problematical things that confront us in the pursuit of our purpose.

Keeping that in mind, notice some very different ways of looking at the Valley of Baca. Some would approach it with little expectation and a negative attitude. There have been no springs there and there will be none for us. Not so with the person whose strength is in the Lord and whose heart is set on pilgrimage. When they pass through the Valley of Baca they make it a spring. Amazing! The joy of being on the way to Jerusalem and the presence of the living God enables them to anticipate blessings where they could least be expected. Their attitude is positive and resilient. Attitudes are our outer expression of our inner purpose.

Note the progression. Those with a pilgrim's heart expect the blessing of the Lord and prayerfully anticipate His intervention. They see springs where there have been no springs! "They make it a spring . . ." (v. 6). That does not mean that they either dug wells or pretended they were there with euphemistic expressions of hope to overcome the negative feelings of others. They simply believed that the Lord would provide.

And the result? ". . . The rain also covers it with pools" (v. 6). The Hebrew word for *pools* has the same consonants as the word *blessings*. The word *blessings* is used in some ancient Hebrew versions. These pilgrims who expected the Lord to care for them were rewarded with rain that blessed them with a quenched thirst and strength to go on to Jerusalem.

Those words hold an exciting meaning for us. Probably one of our greatest hindrances is a limited view of what is possible. God will bless us to the extent of our expectation. He usually gives us no more than we dare to ask. So, if we can't see a spring, or refuse to believe that in its place the Lord will provide something better, we will probably go thirsty. Such an idea is alarming!

Great people are those who, because their pilgrim purpose is to glorify God, can see the potential wrapped up in problems. They ask: What can I learn from this? What is the Lord seeking to teach me? What does He want me to dare to ask and expect?

The greater our purpose, the greater our positive expectation of blessing. When we seek His will and His specific direction of what to pray, He gives us exactly what we need in the problems that confront us. We can unwrap the problem, take it apart, grapple with it as a stepping stone to greater growth, and allow the Lord to show us His solution. Our optimism is not based on our cleverness or the creative skill of others, but on what God can and will do to guide us through the problem.

The Pilgrim's Power

Now we are ready to consider the psalmist's affirmation of the pilgrim's power. "They go from strength to strength . . ." (v. 7). Our experience of the Lord's provision in problems opens us up to greater trust in the future. We can say, "Thank You, Lord. You gave me courage to expect and receive power from You. I know that You will give me greater strength for bigger problems in the future. My purpose is to glorify You in all that happens. The more I face the more You will bless me. Help me to listen for You to tell me what You want and I will claim it." The result is that we become a riverbed for the flow of supernatural strength which perfectly matches the challenges we face.

Think about the problems you're facing right now. In prayer, allow the Lord to give you a picture of what He wants to do to solve those problems. Imagine solutions that would glorify Him in every way, then thank the Lord that it will be so in His timing, way, and strategy. No problem is big enough to keep us from our ultimate purpose of life eternal. That's set and secure. We belong to the

Lord, now and forever, and we can be sure that nothing can happen through any problem that will change our status with Him. Positive optimism based on His faithfulness brings results.

What is the spring in your Valley of Baca? Picture it, claim it, expect it, and wait for its perfectly timed accomplishment.

The five verses that complete the eighty-fourth psalm are a further expression of the psalmist's trust. He has declared his pilgrim purpose, expressed his pilgrim heart, and claimed the pilgrim's power. He confidently reiterates all of these in the closing of his prayer, claiming that he will indeed make it to Jerusalem and the tabernacle of the Lord.

The last two verses are a motto for adventurous living:

> For the LORD God is a sun and shield;
> The LORD will give grace and glory;
> No good thing will He withhold
> From those who walk uprightly.
> O LORD of hosts,
> Blessed is the man who trusts in You!

The psalmist has anticipated our question: Why are some of our prayers seemingly unanswered? He responds, "No *good* thing will He withhold." A good thing is what God determines as ultimately best for us. He answers our prayers with what He withholds as much as what He gives.

Learning how to wait on the Lord has not come easily for me. Often in the past I have thought a problem through, come up with a solution, and asked the Lord for it. If I had received some of those self-propelled plans, the results would have been disastrous. In recent years, I have discovered that the greater part of problem solving is listening long and hard to the Lord before I make my supplication. The difference has been amazing.

The Model of Pilgrimage

We cannot study this psalm without remembering the greatest Pilgrim of all: God with us, Immanuel, Christ our Lord. We wonder if this psalm was on His mind as He set His face to go to Jerusalem. We know that Psalm 118 predicted with awesome detail His triumphal entry, and both the twenty-second and thirty-first psalms were part of the articulation of His prayers on the cross.

I feel confident that verses 8 and 9 of Psalm 84 were like reading His own biography for His Jerusalem:

> O LORD God of hosts, hear my prayer;
> Give ear, O God of Jacob!
> O God, behold our shield,
> And look upon the face of Your anointed.

There is no capitalization of the word *anointed* in this passage, but the Hebrew word *māšîah* has profound prophetic implication as we read it through the eyes of Jesus. In New Testament Greek, *Christos* is translated "(His) Anointed." *The Christ* signified "the Anointed One."

Also in this verse the Hebrew word "shield" *(māgēn)*, was a royal title for the king. Jesus knew He was King of Israel, though a very different kind of king than the people longed for. He also knew He was Messiah and anointed of God to suffer the cross in Jerusalem as the cosmic atonement for sin. He went through His Valley of Baca with firm trust that the worst that could happen in Jerusalem would be the best gift God could give—reconciliation—and the birth of a new creation, the church.

Whenever we face and surrender our problems we remember that. Because of the cross and the resurrection, we are forgiven, justified, and assured of eternal life. In every one of our problems there is a time to die to self-generated cleverness and the illusion of

125

our control. Then, out of the ashes of our burned-out capacities, the Lord resurrects us with an uplifting solution better than our boldest dreams.

In Jesus' Jerusalem we learn about what it means to live as both pilgrim and servant. John observed that the Anointed was so sure of His purpose that He could humble Himself as a servant and wash the disciples' feet:

> Jesus, knowing that the Father had given all things into His hands, and that He had come from God and was going to God, rose from supper and laid aside His garments, took a towel and girded Himself. After that, He poured water into a basin and began to wash the disciples' feet . . . (John 13:3–5).

Following the Example

In a similar way, following the Master's example, a pilgrim's purpose of knowing from whom we have come and where we are going, frees us to express our pilgrim's heart for others. That means giving ourselves away in meeting others' needs. And one of the greatest needs people have, except for salvation itself, is to have a positive friend who walks through life's Valleys of Baca with them and dares to envision springs.

Are we the kind of friend with whom people can share their problems because they know we will have a positive attitude based on the Lord's power? Or are we people who see only the arid, rocky valley and indicate by the way we face our own problems that we don't believe that the Lord intervenes with blessings?

A sure sign that we have a pilgrim's purpose, heart, and power is that our life will be spent lifting up the discouraged and helping the negative. Inside every problem there is an opportunity to be a servant—sometimes, like the Master, to wash the feet of the very people who betray, deny, and misunderstand us. But also like the Master, we know where we are going. Thus we can sing,

Guide me, O Thou great Jehovah,
Pilgrim through this barren land;
I am weak, but Thou art mighty
Hold me with Thy powerful hand.[1]

He has held us, and He will continue to do so, now and forever. To that security, we turn our attention next.

12

Eternal Security
Psalm 90 & 91

We all know the experience of having a disturbing thought on the edge of our minds. We may have an unsolved problem, an unresolved relationship, or haunting memory. Most troublesome of all are our hidden, unexpressed fears They lurk in the corners of our minds, surfacing at times we least expect. They drain our mental and emotional energies, robbing us of peace of mind and full productivity.

A Common Fear

One submerged fear we all have in common. In fact, it is the greatest of all fears and masquerades in lesser fears. We try not to think about it, usually resist facing it, and avoid talking about it. That fear is the fear of death and dying.

A young woman went to the post office. As she turned to leave, a man beside her staggered and fell into her arms. He was dying of a heart attack. When the ambulance arrived, he had died. She had never witnessed death before and was unaware of its gruesome reality.

Afterward, she said, "It was terrible . . . there was nothing I could do. I felt so helpless. I tried to comfort him but couldn't. I wonder if he was ready to die."

Most of us would have to admit we're not ready. We try not to think of death even though we know it'll eventually come to all of us. We put off thinking about it, immersed in the pressure of our everyday affairs.

Death has been called the "king of horrors." We attempt to disguise its stark reality, eventuality, and physical finality with euphemistic circumlocutions and the mortician's handiwork. But the fear won't go away. Each bout with sickness or physical limitation reminds us that there will be a day when we breathe our last breath, our heart will cease beating, and our brain will stop functioning. Failures in life become diminutive deaths, and the terminal illnesses of loved ones and friends shock us again with the fact that we too have an appointment with physical termination on the calendar of eventuality.

Conquering "King Horror"

We can't live with freedom and joy until we've conquered the fear of death, but we can't do that alone. We need a profound healing of our fear, which is based on authoritative truth about the impotence of death to end the eternal life for which we were created. That truth must be more than wishful dreams or a conjectured hunch. No human philosophy of life will suffice. No platitude about our influence continuing after death will satisfy. Not even the best worded theories of immortality and the endless existence of the soul will give solace.

Recently, I received a phone call from a dear friend in the East. She is a member of a church I once served as pastor. Through many visits, I saw her come to an unshakable faith in Jesus Christ as her Lord and Savior. Though she was seldom free from physical pain, she received courage and endurance. Our visits often dealt with death and the confidence she now had that she would not only live forever, but also would know a glorious multiplication of the love, joy, and peace she had begun to experience in her relationship with the Savior.

Her phone call was to tell me that the doctor's prognosis was that she did not have long to live physically. My immediate response was, "Dear friend, I'm sorry." Her reply was amazing. "Please, don't be. I'm ready. These years of knowing the Savior have given me a freedom from the fear of dying. I'm not afraid. I'm going home. I conquered death when I gave my life to Christ. Heaven began then. Now all it can get is better!"

We prayed together on the phone and said our good-byes. Her parting words were, "It's not really good-bye for long. I'll see you in heaven. I'll be there to welcome you home!"

The impact of that call gave perspective to the pressures I was facing that day. The thought of death was moved from the edge to the center of my thinking. With delight I reaffirmed my own conviction that I too would die and that I knew with assurance where I would spend eternity. The problems of the day were tackled with gusto as I claimed again that heaven had also begun for me. I felt at home because of the eternal home that I, too, knew I was destined to enjoy.

How do you feel about that? Do you share that confidence? Do you have a relationship with God that gives you the assurance of abundant life now and forever?

Two Psalms of Refuge

In our quest to live life at full potential, we turn to the ninetieth and ninety-first psalms. They both express that God alone is our dwelling place in the changing, transitory experience of this life. The word *place* in Hebrew—*mā'ôn*—meaning the abode of refuge, protection, and sustenance, had great significance to the Israelites, whose wilderness wanderings were never forgotten and often recounted in their turbulent national life.

Psalm 90 is attributed to Moses, and rightly so, for it expresses the hoped for permanence of God's place for Israel when they reached the fulfillment of the promised land. In response to the instability and brevity of life, God alone was their security and protection.

The same longing for stability in the brief span of the years of this life has made the ninetieth psalm a vibrant source of courage for God's people through the ages. People have repeated its words of comfort in times of turbulence and uncertainty. It has also been a source of solace when they have been confronted with not only the trouble, but also the transience of life.

For that reason, the majestic words of the psalm give comfort as we realize how short our years of physical life are. In times of difficulty as well as death of those we love, we have repeated the words,

> LORD, You have been our dwelling place
>   in all generations.
> Before the mountains were brought forth,
> Or ever You had formed the earth and the world,
> Even from everlasting to everlasting, You are God (vv. 1–2).

Moses' deep conviction that "the eternal God is your refuge" (Deut. 33:27) is sounded triumphantly again in this psalm. The Lord had given the great leader of His people the vision of His eternal nature. He was before all things, and through Him all things were made. Therefore He is the only reliable refuge in the instability of life.

The Long and the Short of It

The psalm goes on to stress God's eternity by comparing it with our brevity. The comparison gives us a stark conviction of the shortness of life but little comfort for the living of it.

> You turn man to destruction,
> And say, "Return, O children of men."
> For a thousand years in Your sight
> Are like yesterday when it is past,
> And like a watch in the night.

You carry them away like a flood;
They are like a sleep.
In the morning they are like grass which grows up;
In the morning it flourishes and grows up;
In the evening it is cut down and withers (vv. 3–6).

Our life compared to the eternity of God is like a second in the ever-rolling waves of time. If a thousand years are like a watch in the night (four hours), what is even a full life lived to old age?

To be sure his readers got the point, the psalmist repeated with specifics:

The days of our lives are seventy years;
And if by reason of strength they are eighty years,
Yet their boast is only labor and sorrow;
For it is soon cut off, and we fly away (v. 10).

The brevity of life is used as an admonition to confess our secret sins and more confidently abide in the dwelling place of the Lord while there is time. But for what reason? The psalm does not promise that coming to God's dwelling place in this life will give us a place for eternity. Rather we are to count carefully the brief number of our days so that we may experience wisdom, the knowledge of God, before we die.

Who knows the power of Your anger?
For as the fear of You, so is Your wrath.
So teach us to number our days,
That we may gain a heart of wisdom (vv. 11–12).

The advice seems to be, "Get cracking! Life is short. Our purpose here on earth is to know God. Our sin mars that possibility. Fear God and get right with Him, for this life is all you have to live in His dwelling place."

133

The psalm closes with the same note of urgency, not in preparation for the next life, but in making the most of this life.

> Oh, satisfy us early with Your mercy,
> That we may rejoice and be glad all our days!
> Make us glad according to the days in
>   which You have afflicted us,
> And the years in which we have seen evil.
> Let Your work appear to Your servants,
> And Your glory to their children.
> And let the beauty of the LORD our God be upon us,
> And establish the work of our hands for us;
> Yes, establish the work of our hands (vv. 14–17).

The message seems to be that difficulties and affliction have been
allowed by God to bring His people to trust only in Him and, while
life lasts, to work for His glory.

Psalm 91 provides magnificent courage for our brief pilgrimage
in this life, but it also offers no promise of any hope beyond death.
Again the place of abiding with God during these years is stressed:

> He who dwells in the secret place of the Most High
> Shall abide under the shadow of the Almighty.
> I will say of the LORD, "He is my
>   refuge and my fortress;
> My God, in Him I will trust" (vv. 1–2).

Having a "place" with God for these years of earthly existence is
not enough! There are eternal longings in our souls, an insatiable
hunger to live beyond the grave—and these feelings are not surprising. God made us that way, and not even the majesty of the language of these promises gives us lasting contentment. We long for a
place with God *now* that gives our souls a place forever. We ache for
an eternal security. The psalms declare the eternity of God and the

shortness of life, and in Christ we discover both the eternity of God and the eternal length of our life.

An Eternal Home

Christ also talked of a dwelling place. He came to prepare a place in our hearts for God and an eternal place in God's heart for us. The psalms press us on to the incarnation, where the dwelling place "in all generations" is revealed to be an eternal dwelling place for each of us. In that context the admonition that we "number our days, that we may gain a heart of wisdom" (Ps. 90:12) takes on new meaning and urgency.

True wisdom is the realization that this life is but a brief phase in the chapter of our life—an inch on the yardstick of eternity. Therefore, discovering a dwelling place in God *now*, becomes the most urgent challenge of life so that when death comes, our dwelling with God does not change. Rather, it is released from earthly, physical limitations for fuller, even more sublime realization.

Our minds rush urgently to the upper room to claim the promise of Christ who said,

> "Let not your heart be troubled; you believe in God, believe also in Me. In My Father's house are many mansions; if it were not so, I would have told you. I go to prepare a *place* for you. And if I go and prepare a place for you, I will come again and receive you to Myself; that where I am, there you may be also" (John 14:1–3, italics added).

Love saturates these words of promise. Repeatedly, Jesus declared the purpose of His life, death, and rising from the dead was so that we "should not perish but have eternal life" (John 3:16). He came to reveal that eternal life, went to the cross to defeat the power of evil and death, rose triumphantly as proof that death had lost its power, and returns to live His life in His people.

A *Place for Us*

In that perspective we consider His promise to prepare a place for us. What He said to the disciples that night in the upper room makes it possible to say God is our dwelling place and to abide in the secret place of the Most High with greater assurance. I often have wondered if Jesus had the ninety and ninety-first psalms and the "dwelling place" on His mind when He spoke those words of comfort. Hope exudes from His description of His own destination and, through Him, the eternal destination of all who live in Him and in whom He lives.

Our Lord's description of heaven includes its nature and expansiveness. "In My Father's house are many mansions . . ." *Father, house, dwellings*—each word sparks our thought and feeling. Whatever else heaven will be, it will be unlimited communion with God. Our partial knowledge of Him will be replaced with free access to Him as His children. *House* defines a quality of family union with our Father and with one another.

In that blessed communion, all that we know here in part will be maximized to the fullest: love, joy, peace, complete satisfaction, and contentment. Think of the most blessed experience you have had of God's presence in your life, multiply it a billion times, and you have some hint of the "glory that shall be revealed in us." *Mansions* means dwellings or rooms. The Greek word is *monai*, plural of *monē*, the noun corresponding with the verb to abide, *menō*. The word *many* simply means that there will be ample room for all the redeemed who have believed in Christ and begun eternal life through salvation in Him while on earth.

The House and the Vine

Linger for a moment on the precious word *dwellings* as *abiding places*. The term takes on greater meaning and significance when we remember that the same Greek word is used for *home* in Jesus' statement recorded in John 14:23: ". . . 'If anyone loves Me, he will keep My word; and My Father will love him, and We will come to him and make Our home with him.'"

Note the difference between that promise and the partial assurance of the two psalms we considered. "God has been our dwelling place." Now our lives are *His* dwelling place! He makes His home in us so that we will be able to make our eternal home in Him. Relationship, companionship, communion are the essence of that indwelling, which prepares us for heaven and makes death only a transition in the midst of eternal life.

But press on to an even more vivid parable of this in John 15. Jesus used the image of the vine and the branches. As the branch must be connected to the vine for life, even so our eternal life is dependent on a consistent fellowship with Him. Again the word for *house, dwelling place,* or *room* is repeated in the verb form. "'Abide in Me and I in you. . . . If you abide in Me and My words abide in you, you will ask what you desire and it shall be done for you" (John 15:4,7). That, indeed, describes the fulfillment of the true nature of the dwelling place we have in God now and forever.

Now we must consider what Christ meant when He said that He would prepare our "place" with God for this life and for eternity. Where did He go to make that preparation? I am convinced that Calvary was that propitious place. Some have suggested He meant His ascension, but merely returning to heaven without the cosmic atonement accomplished would be to return without accomplishing the victory for which He came to earth.

His ascension was with the victory of the cross completed and the enemy of death vanquished. Ephesians 4:8 quotes the messianic promise of Psalm 68:18, "'When He ascended on high, He led captivity captive, and gave gifts to men.'" The vivid picture is of a triumphant, victorious general returning from battle with his defeated enemies staggering behind, stripped of power and devoid of authority.

Jesus' words about the implications of that victory for our eternal life sparkle and flash with infinite meaning: ". . . 'I am the resurrection and the life. He who believes in Me, though he may die, he shall live. And whoever lives and believes in Me shall never die . . .'" (John 11:25). The preparation Jesus made for our eternal dwelling place was to defeat completely the power of Satan, sin, and death over us.

Yet we ask, How does this preparation become real to you and me so we can live without fear? Look at Romans for the apostle Paul's explanation. He clearly stated that Christ died for our sins. When He was crucified, he suffered for our sins to the uttermost. As we have said, sin is essentially separation from God. All sins are the outgrowth of that fractured relationship. Pride, the desire to run our own lives, and all the hurt we cause ourselves and others, are some of the results. When Christ suffered on the cross, He was reconciling us to God and becoming the remittance for our sins.

Baptized into Christ

All this becomes real to us in the recapitulation experience of dying and being raised with Christ.

> Therefore we were buried with Him through baptism into death, that just as Christ was raised from the dead by the glory of the Father, even so we also should walk in newness of life. For if we have been united together in the likeness of His death, certainly we also shall be in the likeness of His resurrection, knowing this, that our old man was crucified with Him, that the body of sin might be done away with, that we should no longer be slaves of sin. For he who has died has been freed from sin. Now if we died with Christ, we believe that we shall also live with Him" (Rom. 6:4–8).

What this means is that when we surrender our lives to Christ and receive the gift of faith to claim His love and forgiveness, we die to self. That spiritual death makes our physical death inconsequential.

In that light, we can understand Paul's concluding thrust in Romans 6. "For the wages of sin is death, but the gift of God is eternal life in Christ Jesus our Lord" (v. 23).

Physical death is frightening only if we face it in a state of separation from God. The reason is that death is the decisive demarcation point. The condition of our spiritual relationship with God at that moment determines where and how we will spend eternity. We all live forever. The question is whether we will live with God in the place prepared for us or separated from Him eternally. Hell is life forever apart from God and all the manifestations of blessings and beauty we take so much for granted during this life. That's the wage, the compensation, for not desiring a relationship with the Lord during the years of this life.

It may seem exclusive to suggest that the place prepared for us is dependent on making the Lord our dwelling place during the years of this life. And yet, what could be more contradictory than claiming an eternity with God which we have not wanted in the years on earth?

Our reluctance to accept death as the demarcation point at which our eternal destination is determined has prompted the development of an antibiblical theory called universalism. The idea is that we are given further opportunity after death to decide whether we want to dwell with the Lord. Put more positively, this theory suggests that God continues His pursuing of our souls all through eternity. Strange theories of an intermediate place have been established for those who haven't decided whether they want to go on to heaven. All that seems absurd in the light of Jesus' urgency for people to believe in Him and receive the assurance of eternal life through Him. Also, it contradicts the inspired Word of God throughout the Bible.

The Crux of the Matter

The time for our decision about eternity is now. Jesus' incisive claim is that, ". . . 'I am the way, the truth, and the life. No one comes to the Father except through Me'" (John 14:6). He is life eternal, the truth of God incarnate, and the only way to God now and at the time of death. His decisive claim is not just that He is the only way to God, but also that He is God's only way of reaching us in our estrangement through sin. Attempting to approach God by bypassing His approach to us is absurd.

When we accept Christ as our Savior we experience our eternal security, which results in an indomitable courage during our years in this life. Christian history is punctuated by the boldness of those who have lived heroically and died gallantly because they knew they were alive forever.

What's important for us is that we can come "home" to the Lord's dwelling place right now and have eternal security about where we will spend eternity. If you have accepted Jesus Christ as your Lord and Savior, invited Him to make His home in you, and allowed Him to prepare you for eternity, you can say with Peter,

Blessed be the God and Father of our Lord Jesus Christ, who according to His abundant mercy has begotten us again to a living hope through the resurrection of Jesus Christ from the dead, to an inheritance incorruptible and undefiled and that does not fade away, reserved in heaven for you, who are kept by the power of God through faith for salvation ready to be revealed in the last time (1 Pet. 1:3–5).

With the fear of death behind us, we can live with security through the days of this life and on into eternity. That makes me want to sing with Isaac Watts,

ETERNAL SECURITY

O God, our help in ages past,
  Our hope for years to come,
Our shelter from the stormy blast
  And our eternal home.

13

Have a Great Day!
Psalm 95

The other morning a friend of mine ended an early morning conversation with the parting shout, "Lloyd, have a great day!" My grateful response was, "Same to you, my friend!"

That started me thinking about what having a great day really means.

Many of us say the words when leaving home in the morning. We want our loved ones to have a good day filled with God's blessings. We end conversations with the phrase throughout the morning, while the day is still young, as a propitious benediction filled with promise.

A Natural Optimism

We all want our days to be great. We awaken with anticipation, plans, and hopes. We long for a particular day to see the resolutions of problems and the triumph over troubles. Our deepest desire is to be efficient and productive. We don't know what the day will bring, but most of us are optimistic enough to believe that a new day will be different from our yesterday.

Our morning prayer is articulated by Samuel Wilberforce:

> Lord, for tomorrow and its needs
> I do not pray;

143

Keep me, my God, from stain of sin
 Just for today.
Let me both diligently work
 And duly pray,
Let me be kind in word and deed
 Just for today.
Let me be slow to do my will,
 Prompt to obey,
Help me to mortify my flesh
 Just for today.
Let me no wrong or idle word
 Unthinking say;
Set Thou a seal upon my lips
 Just for today. . . .

So for tomorrow and its needs
 I do not pray
But keep me, guide me, love me, Lord
 Just for today.[1]

I believe the Lord wants to do exactly that for each of us. Yet do you find, as I do, that your day is often just the opposite, or at least, a mixture of the Lord's effort to make it a great day and our own sometimes confused responses to the pressures of life and the problems of people?

What goes wrong? How can a day that begins with bright expectation so often end in the unfinished, unresolved, and the unpleasant memories of resisting God's best for us? When do we tighten up and become an obstruction to what He wants rather than an enabler of it?

The Heart Is the Issue

I am convinced that the Lord wants to use everything that happens in any one day for our growth and His glory. What happens to and in our hearts in any one day makes the difference. Often what has happened to us in our yesterdays makes our hearts resistant to new possibilities in a new day. And yet, in any day the Lord is impinging on our hearts to fill us with His Spirit, to guide us each step of the way, and to give us supernatural wisdom for any trouble that comes. With that assurance we should be able to

> Forget the past and live the present hour
> Now is the time to work, the time to fill
> The soul with noblest thoughts, the time to will
> Heroic deeds, to use whatever dower
> Heaven has bestowed, to test our utmost power.[2]

But why does that happen to so few of our days? Life does something to our hearts that makes them less than receptive to having a great day.

An insightful teacher told his student, who was later to become a great violinist, "Before you are finished, the world will do one of three things with you. It will make your heart very hard, it will make it very soft, or else it will break it. No one escapes!"

What do you think of that prognosis? Are there only three alternatives? Hardness, softness, or the breaking of the heart? Our own experience would confirm it. Life has made some of us hard as we've faced trouble. Others have found that suffering has mysteriously made us kind, tender, and empathetical with others. Still others feel their hearts have been broken by what people and circumstances have done to us. Trouble has a way of producing greatness or grimness.

Understanding Our Hearts

In this chapter I want to talk about our hearts. My purpose is to discover how to overcome heartbreaking experiences so that our hearts become soft and not hard, so that our life can be a succession of great days.

The *heart*, in the Hebrew sense used in the Psalms, means our intellect, will, and emotions—that inner dimension which affects the person we become outwardly. Our capacity to think, decide, and express emotions is the point of contact we have with the Spirit of God. With our hearts we can comprehend the greatness of God, decide to do great things for Him and by His power, and become great people who are able to express His love, forgiveness, and compassion.

So often today we speak figuratively of our hearts as a synonym for feeling and our heads as our intellect. Hebrew would not reflect that kind of dichotomy. We are a unified whole. What happens in our thinking affects what is implemented by our wills and expressed by our emotions.

When we say a person has a "hard heart" we usually mean that he or she is unfeeling, or when a person has a "soft head" that his or her thinking is not solid and based on firm convictions. These designations would be foreign to the Hebrew of the Scriptures.

Soft thinking can produce a hard heart, however, and constricted feelings can result in rigid thought patterns. Our desire is to discover wholeness in which our thought, will, and emotions are under the control and guidance of the Spirit.

Throughout the rest of this chapter, I will be speaking of the heart in this broader, more inclusive sense. My goal is for us to avoid either soft heads or hard hearts. Rather, when life presents its usual blend of delights and difficulties we can gain the Lord's perspective, receive His power to do His will, and become channels of His passion in the expression of emotional warmth and joy.

A *Psalm for the Heart*

In Psalm 95:7–8, we are given an admonition on how to do that: "Today, if you will hear His voice:/'Do not harden your hearts . . .'" This statement is the fulcrum of the whole psalm.

The first seven verses call us to unfettered praise and the last four to unrestrained obedience. J. H. Jowett said, "An act of worship is intended to hallow the life. It is not a fleeting bit of ritualism, a spasm of homage which passes with the hour. It is purposed to be the experience of a mood in which everything in life is to be sanctified."[3]

Note how the psalm prepares us to do that. Praise is to prepare us to have supple, receptive hearts for what the Lord wants to say in any day of our lives. Here's a way to begin a great day.

> Oh come, let us sing to the LORD!
> Let us shout joyfully to the Rock of our salvation.
> Let us come before His presence with thanksgiving;
> Let us shout joyfully to Him with psalms.
> For the LORD is the great God,
> And the great King above all gods (vv. 1–3).

The psalmist follows this call to praise the Lord with the motivation of that adoration. The Lord is creator and sustainer of all. Then, with that thought in mind, he turns to the crucial necessity of trusting our needs to the Shepherd of our lives.

> Oh come, let us worship and bow down;
> Let us kneel before the LORD our Maker.
> For He is our God,
> And we are . . . the sheep of His hand (vv. 6–7).

All that praise and adoration of the Lord may begin a great day, but something more is needed to realize the Lord's blessing through the day. Saying, "We must seek the Lord in the morning if we want Him through the day" is one thing, but it is quite another to say, "We must be open to the Lord all through the day if we want to do things His way." A great day is seeking the Lord's way all through the day.

How to Seek God's Will

Verse 8 of this ninety-fifth psalm gives us the secret of how to do that. "Today, if you will hear His voice: 'Do not harden your hearts. . . .'"

There are three aspects of that admonition that give us the basis of living a great day and provide a progression for our thought. We must ask three questions: Who speaks? When do we listen? What do we do? Here is the who, when, and what of dynamic communication with God in prayer all through the day.

Who Speaks?

The psalmist answers, "His voice"—the voice of the One whom we have praised in the first half of the psalm. He is the Creator, Lord, King and great Shepherd of all time, every day, and each circumstance. Most of all, He is *our* God. Our times, each day, are in His hand. Robert Browning caught the urgency of listening to the Lord. God must be able to shape us each day into the person He intends us to be, for an eternal day in which there will be neither dawns nor sunsets, but a timeless communion in heaven.

> So, take and use Thy work:
> Amend what flaws may lurk,
> What strain o' the stuff, what warpings past the aim!
> My times are in Thy hand!
> Perfect the cup as planned!
> Let age approve of youth, and death complete the same![4]

That our God knows us and wants to speak to us is a source of awe and wonder. He is the divine Artificer in the shaping of our lives. Each day we yield the "cup" of our hearts for His molding. He speaks, and we are to listen, act, and express the emotional response to what we hear.

148

The astounding aspect of this truth is that the Lord speaks. He is the initiator and instigator of the relationship. Out of sheer grace He comes to us, with His word of interpretation on the triumphs and troubles of life and His intervention of infusing power to do His will. A great day is one in which we listen for Him all through the day and respond to what He says. The fact that the Lord speaks and we can hear says a majestic thing about His love for us and a magnificent thing about our created nature to be receivers and transmitters of His mind.

An eminent scientist in my congregation said something to me the other evening which exemplifies how the Lord speaks. "I start the day praising the Lord for His divine intelligence. He knows all things and the secrets of the universe. Then throughout the day in my investigations and subsequent scientific writing, I repeatedly yield to His guidance for the order and content of my thoughts. He uses me to expose the truth about us and life. When the day ends, I realize I've had a great day because He has actually thought through my mind."

The discoveries this man has made have radically changed the practice of medicine in America. He listens; God speaks.

The Lord speaks through inspiration of thought, through circumstances, and sublimely through the Scriptures. When we are receptive we can hear what He is saying to us through the events of the day. When we are consistent in reading the Bible, He wondrously leads us to passages that speak to what He wants to teach us in joys and sorrows.

So often people open conversations with me by saying, "I don't know what the Lord is trying to tell me in all this!" My task then, as with myself in similar quandaries, is to ask, "What do you need to hear?" Usually their need is a word of comfort, assurance, or courage.

Often, we know in our hearts that we need a corrective word. We need to trust Him and not the circumstances or our ability to manipulate things to work out for our good. There are times when failure convicts us of the ineffective way we've been running our own lives and our need to confess our imperious self-will. A difficulty can be transformed in the moment in any day by saying with Samuel, "Speak, LORD, for Your servant hears" (1 Sam. 3:9).

The other day I visited with a woman whose husband has been infected with a crippling illness. Our conversation reviewed all the good years she had had in their marriage. The questions of "Why did this happen to us now?" yielded to, "How can the Lord help me face this and be what my husband needs me to be?" Finally, we had to deal with the eventuality of sickness, God's power to heal in His way and timing, and most of all, His availability to be her only security in a radically altered life-style. If she lost everything, the Lord would not forsake her. That renewed assurance gave her courage.

The Lord spoke through our conversation and prayers that day. As a result she was given the gift of trusting faith to live each day to the fullest rather than have her hours blighted with the "what might have beens."

What happened to that woman in that crisis, is what the Lord wants to happen all through our days in the big and the little troubles of life. Asking "What do You have to say, Lord?" opens us to receive perspective and power.

The same is true of the successes and delights of any day. Our temptation is to take credit for the good things and forget to praise the Lord, and then to blame Him for the difficulties without asking what He wants us to learn. Again, I want to emphasize the importance of discovering in each day what the impact should be on our hearts of the gracious things the Lord does. He knits our victories into the faith fabric of our capacity to trust Him in the future. If we discover how to give Him the credit all through the day, we become expectant, vibrant people.

The Listening Ear

The second emphasis of verse 8 of this ninety-fifth psalm is in answer to the question, "When shall we hear?" *Today!* is the psalmist's response. We are challenged with the urgency of listening now. William Manson, the great biblical scholar of another generation, used to say, "Every day of delay leaves a day more to repent of, and a day less to repent in."

Building on that, I say every day of delay leaves a day more to repent of, and a day less in which to rejoice. Delay piles up the unconfessed sins and the unacknowledged blessings. We become what we do not express in response to what the Lord has said. Today becomes a repeat of yesterday. A succession of yesterdays in which we have not listened ends up in a whole life of failures and unexpressed praise.

Life is given us in day-tight compartments. Living each day as if it were our only day makes for a total life lived at full potential.

Today is the day in which to do what we are tempted to put off till tomorrow. If we have never surrendered our lives completely to the Lord, today is the day. We may not have a tomorrow. If we have longed for a Spirit-filled and -guided life, today is the day to start. When we don't, there is one fewer day to enjoy living at the maximum in the flow of the Lord's power. If we have hung on to problems, trying desperately to solve them ourselves, today is the day to resign as the manager of our lives and turn the reins of power over to the Lord.

The first day of the evolving solution to these problems is today. If our lives have drifted from day to day in dull sameness, then today is the day to begin praising the Lord in all circumstances. If we have known the Lord's guidance for some broken relationship or some pattern of action, today is the day to stop in our tracks, ask for guidance and strength, and do what we've put off. The beginning of a new life starts now!

I like the way the apostle Paul concluded his description in 2 Corinthians 5:12—6:2 of the new creation made possible by Christ's death and resurrection, and the new creatures we can become as agents of reconciliation. He offers a bold invitation: ". . . Behold, now is the accepted time; behold, now is the day of salvation" (6:2). That could be the motto for us who want to have a great day.

An Appropriate Response

How to do that is described in the third aspect of our text, "Today, if you will hear His voice: 'Do not harden your hearts. . . .'" The verse also tells us what not to do in any one day to make it great. "Do not harden your hearts."

What is a hardened heart? It is the intellectual rigidity, the volitional obstinance, and the emotional unresponsiveness that blocks what the Lord has to say to us in any day. Our first reaction is amazement. How could anyone not want to listen to the Lord of all creation, the Lord of the love of the cross, the Lord of the victory of the resurrection, and the Lord of indwelling power released at Pentecost? Such stubbornness does seem absurd, doesn't it? But people do succumb to it; we do often; I do repeatedly.

There's a difference between temporary hardness and a more solidified attitude of hardness. Many of us drift into the experience by a series of choices not to trust the Lord, or life dishes out a long succession of disappointments and we get discouraged.

Also, people around us can hurt us so much we steel ourselves against being hurt further. To protect ourselves, we make ourselves resistant and impervious to the good that happens as well as the bad. Our hearts become temporarily overlayed with the hard crust of defensiveness. For this condition, we need the alarming realization that our days are slipping by in the prison of aloneness, while we sit and nurse our hurts. We and the people around us are robbed of the flow of love, joy, affirmation, and delight in life we were meant to communicate. Most of all, we cut ourselves off from the Lord and His help.

The more solidified attitude of hardness comes when we stiff-arm God for so long that we no longer think about our need for Him or our desire to do His will. We become addicted to the habit of living our days on our own strength and grim determination.

The psalmist had a ready example of this, which every Hebrew remembered from his or her history. The rest of Psalm 95 describes the rebellion of the people of Israel in the wilderness during the Exodus from Egypt. The Lord liberated them from bondage in Egypt and then on the trek to the Promised Land sought to liberate them from the bondage of fear The first incident, including the opening of the Red Sea and the repeated miracles to release Israel from Pharaoh's grasp, was easier to go through in faith than the second. Fear hardened the hearts of the people at Rephidim. They murmured against the Lord about the lack of water and He gave them drink from the rock (see Ex. 17:1–7). Moses named the place Meribah, which means "contention."

All through the forty years of wandering in the wilderness, the people were hardened to God's guidance. He did not intend that they would be in the wilderness for forty years. In fact, fourteen months after their release from Egypt, after they had witnessed repeated signs of the Lord's intervention and had received the gift of the Ten Commandments on Sinai, they were led to the edge of Canaan (see Num. 13–14).

Remember the account: Spies were sent in to survey the land. The majority of them came back with frightening tales of the presence of the fearsome tribes of Anak. The minority report by Caleb and Joshua was that the land was flowing with milk and honey. "Let us go in and possess the land!" they said with God-inspired confidence, but the hardened hearts of the people equivocated and eventually they refused to dare to trust the Lord. The result was that they wandered about in the wilderness, to and fro in a relatively small area of land, because they lacked courage to claim the Lord's promise.

Only after thirty-eight more years of wandering did they finally grasp the Lord's assurance of power and enter the land of Canaan under Joshua's inspiring leadership. The historic event became parabolic of the human tendency to proclivity and procrastination. A whole generation missed the Promised Land because they hardened their hearts.

One of the most alarming analyses of this hardness of heart in the wilderness is given in Psalm 106:15: "And He gave them their request, but sent leanness into their soul." Other translations put it, "He gave them the desires of their hearts, but sent leanness into their souls." The frightening aspect of the lesson is that God honors the gift of will He has given us. He created us with freedom to will to do His will. The major cause of hardness of heart is when the will becomes the master rather than the implementor of thought. The emotional outbursts of resistance or rebellion are expressed in murmurings of complaint against God.

Another striking biblical example of this is in the Pharisees who rejected Jesus. He accused them of hardness of heart. His claim to be Messiah and His resolute call to seek first the kingdom of God was an exposure of their resistance to the very God whom they were organized to serve. They ridiculed Jesus' miracles, accused Him of being possessed with Satan, and became part of the collusive plot to kill Him. Mark 3:5 tells us that Jesus "looked around at them with anger, being grieved by the hardness of their hearts" when He sought to care for the man with a withered hand.

When they challenged Jesus about Moses' regulation on divorce, He noted hardness of heart as the chief cause of Moses' having to allow a certificate of divorce (see Mark 10:3–6).

In Mark 16:14 we see that hardness of heart was not limited to the Pharisees. After the resurrection, Jesus appeared to the disciples "and rebuked their unbelief and hardness of heart, because they did not believe those who had seen Him after He had risen." Only after Pentecost was the tendency to hardness of heart transformed by Christ's indwelling Spirit. Even then He had to work with them constantly to keep them flexible and open to His agenda for them. As they faced the Gentile world, the early Christians had to admit and confess their hardness of heart concerning non-Hebrews. The church would have survived as little less than a sect of Judaism if the Lord had not persisted in softening their rigid exclusivism.

What does all this mean for us who are longing to have a succession of great days as a part of a lifetime of greatness? We must ask ourselves some questions. Is there any area where we are resisting the Lord? Does He have complete control over the intellectual, volitional, and emotional capacities of our hearts? Have the hurts of life been endured in self-pity and self-justification instead of listening to His voice speaking love, forgiveness, and acceptance of the shortcomings of others? Hurts will make us hard, and we will end up hurting ourselves by denying ourselves the healing we need today and for eternity.

Are we willing to make today the first day of a new beginning? Start by praising the Lord in the words of this magnificent ninety-fifth psalm. Then get on your knees and give the day to Him. Our hearts can be broken only if they become hard. A supple heart can be shaped but not broken.

In M. E. Waller's *Woodcarver of 'Lympus*, a woman said, "Before I knew it, Hugh, I was dropping my anchor, losing the clear, sweet, childlife faith I had kept as my heart heritage from my father and mother, and with it, losing all of the spontaneous joy of life."[5]

Today, not tomorrow, is the day to pull up the anchor and begin a new life. Give the Lord your heart. Tell Him you don't want another day of hardening but a new day of ready responsiveness.

In the light of that truth, I really mean it: Have a great day!

14

A Case for Gladness
Psalm 100

There are times that we take ourselves and our service to the Lord so seriously that we lose the gladness of our faith. We become grim. That's when we need the one hundredth psalm, one of the shortest in the Psalter, as an antidote. The psalm makes a strong case for gladness as the sure sign that we are living by grace and not our efforts. We are reminded that God is in charge, that we belong to Him, and that His mercy is everlasting. Here's a psalm to read when you're down and need a bracing tonic for your soul.

> Make a joyful shout to the LORD,
>   all you lands!
> Serve the LORD with gladness;
> Come before His presence with singing.
> Know that the LORD, He is God;
> It is He who has made us,
>   and not we ourselves;
> We are His people
>   and the sheep of His pasture.
> Enter into His gates with thanksgiving,
> And into His courts with praise.
> Be thankful to Him, and bless His name.
> For the LORD is good;
> His mercy is everlasting,
> And His truth endures to all generations.

These five verses, made up of eighty-five words, should be memorized and repeated every morning. They will clarify our purpose and change our attitude toward the way we serve the Lord in any day. This psalm could change your life, for it has mine. The way it happened was very humorous. I can still remember it as if it had happened last Sunday.

Taking Ourselves Too Seriously

When I was a young clergyman, I took myself and my responsibilities far too seriously. There was little gladness, especially when I led worship. I was overly impressed with my Scots Presbyterian heritage. The completion of my education at the University of Edinburgh gave me far too much pride. I became sort of a "professional Scot" when I conducted worship. Everything was done "decently and in order."

I wore all the accoutrements of Scottish clerical garb: a clerical collar, preaching tabs, cassock, academic robe and hood, and when I could get away with it, even a Calvin clergy hat. I had so much on I had difficulty gesturing when I preached. I was a study of black-robed dignity, indeed! When I would follow the choir down the aisle in a very formal processional I would parade in peacock fashion, my black robes swaying majestically to my rhythmic steps.

At that time my oldest son, Scott, was a little boy. His hero was Zorro, the masked bandit who wore black boots, cape, hat, and brandished a silver sword. Scott had acquired the whole costume and loved to act out all of the feats of Zorro gallantry he had watched on television. One Sunday as I marched down the aisle in all my assumed and acquired clerical dignity, he was seated on the end of a pew, right next to the aisle. Just before I reached his pew, he hopped up, flashed his hand as if it had a trusty sword in it, and said with gusto, "Zorro!"

I started to laugh. My son thought I looked like Zorro! That made me laugh all the more at myself and how seriously I had taken myself as a leader in the worship of God. He had used a boy's undecorous act to help me see what was happening to me.

I led the rest of the service still laughing inside. Only the people right around him had seen what he had done, but the whole congregation sensed a difference in me. When I greeted the congregation following worship, people said, "You've never seemed happier in the service of worship. You smiled and seemed so relaxed. Best sermon we've heard you preach!"

I didn't tell them why. That would have spoiled a special moment between a son and his dad. But the way I felt in that service, and the positive comments of people afterward, alarmed me with the realization that I needed to take myself less seriously and discover how to enjoy the Lord. He had begun to pry open the lid of my "piousity." And He's not finished. Often, I have to be reminded that joy is the outward sign of the inner experience of grace. Gladness, not grimness, is the distinguishing mark of anyone who is truly thankful for the goodness of the Lord.

A Growth of Gladness

That experience years ago began a long process of growth in gladness in my life. The clerical garb was not the problem, but the false security and fictitious seriousness it provided to cover my timorous heart. I still wear a robe when I lead worship, but praise God, it's not a substitute for gladness. I don't need the peacock feathers or plumes anymore!

The evidence of true worship and service is gladness. Anything we can't do with gladness, probably should not be done. Yet so often we live our faith with a dutiful sense of *ought*. We pray because good Christians *ought* to talk to God. We often serve in the church or areas of need in our communities with a strained sense of obligation, or we "pay" our tithe because it's required rather than out of an uncontainable, overflowing gratitude.

A friend of mine who is a clergyman says that he will continue to be a leader in the church only so long as he can perform his responsibilities with gladness. I like that! When I visited his church recently, I found that his spirit of gladness had been contagious. The congregation is doing more to convert people and right social wrongs in the community than most churches I've observed; yet, all the witnessing and social service is done with delight.

Another friend of mine who is a vice president of a large bank always answers any request with five powerful words, "Glad to be of service." That's more than an assumed public relations attitude. He's a Christian and views his work as a crucial aspect of his ministry. He believes that his daily contact with people provides him a fortuitous opportunity to share his faith. Instead of assuming the punitive parent image so many bankers communicate, he feels that helping people with gladness is his calling.

Ministry for All

My church in Hollywood encourages every member to go into the ministry. By that I do not mean that we want all our people to become clergy. We believe that every Christian has a ministry to lead others to Christ and to become involved in some area of social need in the community. We are convinced that our church should be an equipping center for their ministry, and one of the qualifications for that ministry is a spirit of gladness. The psalmist's admonition to serve the Lord with gladness is a constantly reiterated motto.

When people ask me how many ministers we have at the Hollywood Presbyterian Church, my response is, "About five thousand!" I emphasize that knowing the living Christ is a call to a ministry of gladness.

Everyone who has experienced salvation has a threefold ministry. We all have a ministry of prayer as the priests of the Lord. Every Christian has power to intercede for people and then bring His power and love to the people for whom he or she has prayed.

Second, we have a ministry of communication. We have the

joyous opportunity to introduce others to Christ and to share what He can do with the raw material of our problems.

The third aspect of the ministry of all Christians follows naturally. We are called to become involved in areas of social suffering, to bring Christ's healing and hope. However, unless all three can be done with gladness, our efforts will be debilitated by an officious "oughtness." All the people about whom we are concerned have an inalienable right to expect that our efforts to be of service will be done with gladness. Anything less will contradict what we say and try to do.

I sense a kind of love-hate syndrome in the service of many Christians. People are put off. We say we love the Lord, and we serve Him with grim determination. People catch the impact of our attitudes more than our words.

An Attitude of Gratitude

The psalmist has given us the motive for true gladness—gratitude. This one hundredth psalm exudes uncontainable thanksgiving and praise for the Lord Himself and all He has done. The best gift we can give others is to recapture the goodness of the Lord for us. That will overflow in a joyous attitude and countenance that will inspire and encourage others.

I have discovered that serving people and their needs in my own strength is impossible. The secret is to serve them as if serving Christ. His words about our ministry guide our attitudes. "'. . . "Assuredly, I say to you, inasmuch as you did it to one of the least of these My brethren, you did it to Me"'" (Matt. 25:40). There's the secret of service with gladness! In the lonely, frustrated, troubled, and sick of the world, we meet Him. What we do should be done as if we were doing it to Him.

That's no less true of our responsibilities and opportunities in marriage, the family, among our friends, at church, or at work. How often we are less than we would be to Christ! I don't know about you, but that fills me with lots of troublesome memories of what I've said or done that is less than I would have said or done for the Master. But that's done and forgiven. Today is the issue, and for that, He gives us His own Spirit.

Not only are we to serve others as serving Christ, but we are to do so with His Spirit indwelling us. He is the instigator and initiator of serving Him with gladness. That service is done in the shadow of the cross, in the power of Pentecost, and in the effusion of a supernatural power that far exceeds our own resources.

Paul challenged Christians to do all things as to the Lord. He said they were to be known as the servants of the Lord and stewards of His mysteries. Our purpose and power are defined. We are freed from the "I'll help you if you help me" syndrome we work so gingerly in our relationships. That's horizontal living. But when we are constantly amazed by the Lord's love for us, we can communicate unqualified love to others.

Focus on the opportunities you have to serve and to be Christ's love to the people in your life. Make a list. Begin with those most intimately associated with you; then add those the Lord has put on your agenda in your church, at work, or in the community. Picture in your mind what you would look like, how you would act, the tone of your voice, and the willingness of your desire to help. Now hold that image. Ask the Lord to help you do all you do with gladness. Be sure of this: people will be astounded. They'll say, "What happened? There's a gladness about you I've never felt before!"

When you feel misused or put upon, think of the One who loved, gave, suffered, and died that He might liberate you to enjoy serving others in His name and by His power. Suddenly, our attitudes change and we can't wait to get on to the challenges ahead.

Serving with Gladness

A. J. Cronin tells a wonderful story of a nurse in Wales who poured herself out for the needs of people with little or often no pay.

A doctor exclaimed, "Oh, dear nurse, God knows you are underpaid!"

The nurse smiled and her eyes twinkled as she responded, "All I need to know is that God knows."

That's all any of us needs to know. We don't serve for human recognition or approbation. If we do, we will constantly feel unappreciated.

Service with gladness is marked by availability, affirmation, and altruism. When we surrender our schedules to the Lord, He makes us available to people who need His love. What they need is for us to be free enough from our own need for approbation that we can affirm them as cherished people, valued by us and the Lord. There's no room for an obligatory "have to" spirit of grimness in that. Out of authentic affirmation of people will come a trust in which they will be free to share their needs. When those are identified, we discover how to put our caring into practical action. What do we have to lose? Everything we have and are is a gift from the Lord for ministry to others!

Not Settling for the Luxury of Gloom

The final truth Psalm 100 reveals to us is that gladness is not really an option. The sense of the whole psalm is admonition. But what if we don't happen to feel glad? My response is, let's fight our way through our moods to gladness. Gloomy moods are a symptom of a need for fresh grace. Let's ask the Lord for a renewed experience of His love and forgiveness, and that will be the first step to gladness.

Unpleasant moods are a projection of what's on our minds and in our hearts. Often they are the result of feeling neglected, hurt, or misunderstood, or they fester in the mire of unexpressed feelings about what life has done or failed to do for us. We are Christ's people, called to resign from the "me generation." We have been commissioned to be channels of joy and hope. The undeniable test of our Christianity is that we are identified by a contagious gladness.

A young man in my congregation identified a wonderful change in his mother. Recently, she faced what was happening to her family because of her nasty attitude toward her family. Everything she did made her husband and her three sons feel guilty. They could never thank her enough to satisfy her. Whatever they did to express appreciation, she always lodged a knock of "poor mom" in their souls.

Then, at a retreat, she had a profound experience of Christ's love and asked to be filled with His Spirit for her ministry in her home. When she returned home she did the same tasks she had done before, but she did them with gladness. Her son said, "Wow, I've got a new mom! What happened to her at that retreat? I've never seen her so happy. The whole atmosphere around our home has changed. No more put-downs. She's actually fun to be with!" No wonder he felt that way. She was relating to him as if to Christ, and doing it with the indwelling power of His Spirit.

I love the story about missionaries in Africa who presented Christ's love and joy to a distant tribe. One of the chieftains said, "Oh, I know the man you've been talking about. We have seen him. He has been here with us." The chieftain was talking about David Livingstone, who had ministered among them. When Christ was described to him, he immediately identified Him with Livingstone.

Oh, to be that kind of person! We can, by serving the Lord and the people He gives us, with gladness.

15

Rejuvenated Exuberance
Psalm 103

The word *renewal* has worked its way into the fabric of our language in the church today. We speak of the need for spiritual renewal, we hold renewal conferences, and we hear the call for the renewal of purpose and vitality of denominational programs and structures. We need to define what we mean by renewal and discover how it happens to individuals and churches.

Recently, the pastor and officers of a church in another city invited me to lead what they called a "renewal conference." Though I thought I knew what they implied by the words, I asked for an explanation of what they meant by *renewal* and why they had selected that word as an explanation of the need in their church. The response was very revealing and prompted my desire to accept the invitation.

"Our church is filled with good people who have lost the enthusiasm of their faith," the pastor wrote. "Everything, including worship, has become business as usual. There's a blandness about the church. We go through the motions, but there's no sense of movement. Our theology is orthodox, the organization of the church is in keeping with the denomination's plan, and the budget is met every year.

"What's lacking is joy. Perhaps I'm the cause. I can't seem to engender any excitement, any exuberance. There's little evangelism because of this. The church is not growing, even though there are hundreds of potential members in the area. Mission giving is down, and there seems to be little concern for problems in the community where we could make a difference."

The pastor's description of his church could be applied to thousands of churches in America today. Many of them would not have the advantage of this leader's honesty and nondefensive analysis, but the fact remains that contemporary Christians, and often their churches, desperately need renewal.

Starting Out with Number One

The few days spent with this particular church were very rewarding. I began with the pastor. He needed a friend with whom he could express his frustrations. After a time of analyzing his parish, our conversation became very personal. He realized that the renewal of his people had to begin with him. He was a good man with a gift for the pastoral care of his people.

The problem, however, was that his day-and-night availability was taking its toll on his own time for study and refreshment with the Lord. Because his members assumed little responsibility for each other, the total load of counseling and care was on his shoulders. The schedule he had kept had strained his marriage and was depleting his health. Inside the man there was a caldron of anxiety and hidden fears. He was afraid to share with his officers how he felt. He assumed he had to be the bastion of spiritual strength for them.

After hours of conversation, we prayed together. He confessed his own need for the Lord in the depth of his life. In committing his needs and his frustration over his parish to the Lord, a deep healing began. He experienced the Lord's love for him as a person and became a channel of His strength, able to dare to be vulnerable with his officers.

On to the Board

When we met with the officers, the pastor was free to confess his own spiritual and physical exhaustion. He told the leaders how much he needed them. His honesty enabled them to talk openly about their own needs. After a day of Bible study about the abundant life in the flow of Christ's Spirit, these officers saw the need to allow Him to deal with the inner emptiness in their own lives. Many had problems that had never been confessed either to the Lord or to their fellow leaders.

In small groups, these dutiful but spiritually depleted people confessed their need for new life. Their aching need was to recapture the excitement of an adventure in Christ. Some had never made a commitment of their lives to Christ and had been trying to lead the church with only some vague cultural idea of what a congregation should be.

By the end of the time together, they were ready to consider daring biblical goals for their church, which they could not accomplish without the enabling power of the Lord. Their greatest problem had been that they constricted their church's life much as they had their own individual lives. The Lord removed the cap on their reservations. Their personal renewal, through a commitment to the Lord of all that was within them, brought release and an invigorated vision for what could happen in their church if they planned around the Lord's goals and depended on His supernatural power to accomplish them. The Lord had renewed them and their pastor. Now it was time to turn to the congregation as a whole.

Then, the Congregation

In a series of three meetings, the congregation gathered for worship, Bible study, and small group discussion. I felt led to go back to basics, preaching the grace of the Lord, the cross, what it means to live the abundant life, and the secret of Christ's indwelling power. The longing in the people for new life was amazing.

The Lord had honored the pastor's willingness to be open and the officers' freedom to confess their need to be set aflame with vision and daring. Their witness to what was happening to them gave authenticity to what I was trying to explain about renewal. Because I was an outsider, I could say some incisive things about what happens to religious people when they receive the healing of the Lord for their needs.

The significant result was that many who had unrelinquished inner tension and problems released them to the Lord. Marriages were healed, broken relationships were reconciled, hidden hurts were confessed, and determined willfulness was surrendered.

At the closing service of the renewal conference, I asked people to come forward to kneel on the chancel steps to open their minds and hearts to the Lord and receive His Spirit for their problems and potentials. The service went late into the night, as church members came to confess their desire to make a fresh start with the Lord.

What happened that night was only a beginning. The pastor was liberated to preach more boldly than ever before. The officers continued to grow in their new joy. They met weekly for Bible study and prayer and to plan for a vision for their church only the Lord could help them realize. The congregation was organized into small groups to study the Book of Acts. These became caring, enabling groups, which helped those who had come alive in the conference to go on in the adventure of the abundant life.

The result has been a lifting of the burden of pastoral care. People have been ministering to each other. The emphasis of the conference—that every Christian is a minister—took hold. Many became involved in personal evangelism, and the church has begun to grow again. Task-force groups have been organized to deal with social needs in the community. This church is being renewed!

A Widespread Phenomenon

That's not an isolated success story. What is happening in that church is happening in parishes all over America. Perhaps it's happening in your congregation. I'm thankful to say it is happening in our church in Hollywood, but no one conference for renewal will suffice. Renewal must be an ongoing process. One stage of growth prepares us for launching into further stages of new life.

Every week as I look out over my congregation, I know that there are hundreds of people who desperately need a fresh touch of the Lord's Spirit, a new surrender of problems and frustrations, and an experience of rejuvenated exuberance. Only as they are given an opportunity to confess those needs honestly and surrender them to the Lord, will worship or any class or group meeting in the church fulfill its purpose. We dare not take people for granted.

We've all had times of renewal in our spiritual lives. They came at times when our relationship with the Lord had grown perfunctory and lacked enthusiasm. When some problem brought us to the end of our resources or some opportunity beyond our wisdom or strength arrived, we were forced to realize how much we needed the Lord's help. Perhaps we came to realize the needs of the people around us.

Then too, another person whose relationship with the Lord was so radiant and joyful could have caused us to see how much we were missing. One of the greatest gifts the Lord can give us is to make us realize our emptiness. Then in our own prayers, or in a profoundly personal conversation with a trusted friend, we are able to admit our need for renewal.

Often the Lord uses the teaching and preaching of someone who is personal enough to share how the Lord has worked in similar times of blandness in his or her own life. A source of renewal for me is a Bible study and prayer group where we talk about anything that may be keeping us from the flow of the Lord's power. Then we are challenged to take the next step in what the Lord has revealed in His strategy for us.

Whatever the method of getting through to us the Lord uses, He is constantly seeking to move our attention away from ourselves. Then we feel again the joy and delight of our first experience of becoming a Christian. The time of renewal puts the Lord back on center stage of the unfolding drama of our lives. His Spirit creates a new hunger for reading the Bible, a new openness to the invasions of His grace in our impossibilities, and a new readiness to discover and do His will. We think we will never be the same again.

Yet, before long we are! The months go by and soon we drift back into dullness. The demands of living edge out the renewed commitment and things return to their lackluster sameness, or we live out to the fullest what the previous renewal time had taught us and life levels off on a plane of unadventuresome living again.

A Psalm of Repeated Renewal

How can we discover a secret of ever-renewing spiritual life? How can we get off the cycle of ups and downs of excitement about the Lord and dull toleration of Him? What would it take to keep our faith fresh and vigorous all the time?

Psalm 103 contains the key to daily renewal. This psalm of triumphant praise has a residual power in it that can bring rejuvenated exuberance to our spiritual life. What the psalmist discovered at a time of particular blessing in his life can be the source of constant refreshment for us. He had been through a perilous experience of weakness and physical disability, which had brought him to the brink of death. The Lord intervened and gave him a new beginning. In response, he marshaled all his capacities to bless the Lord for His forgiveness, the healing of diseases, the gift of a new beginning, and all the bonuses of His lovingkindness. The psalmist claimed the result of those blessings from the Lord. His youth was renewed like the eagle's.

Verses 1 and 5 of the psalm belong together. They are two parts of the renewing experience. The antidote to bland spirituality is, "Bless the LORD, O my soul; and all that is within me, bless His holy name! . . ./So that your youth is renewed like the eagle's." To bless the Lord with all that is within us does renew our lives with rejuvenated exuberance spiritually, emotionally, and physically. Let's consider in depth how this works.

The salient portion of the psalmist's admonition to himself was to bless the Lord not only with his soul, but with all that was within him. As a sensitive Hebrew, he had repeated often Moses' words in Deuteronomy 6:5, "'You shall love the LORD your God with all your heart, with all your soul, and with all your might.'" Could it be that, in the light of this ancient command to love the Lord with all his capacities, the psalmist was calling his heart and might into blessing the Lord?

The words *all that is within me* mean "all my inward parts." Calvin points this out in his exposition of these verses of the psalm.

> Not content with calling upon his soul (by which he unquestion-ably means the seat of the understanding and the affections) to bless God, the prophet expressly adds *inward parts*, addressing as it were his own mind and heart, and all the faculties of both. When he thus speaks to himself, it is as if, removed from the presence of men, he examined himself before God. The repeti-tion renders his language still more emphatic, as if he thereby intended to reprove his own slothfulness.[1]

The soul is the spirit within us capable of receiving the Lord's Spirit. It is the way of entry of the Holy Spirit, the threshold of His invasion of our total inner self. Jesus affirmed this when he said, "God is Spirit, and those who worship Him must worship in spirit and truth" (John 4:24). The spirit in us is meant to be the contact point with the Lord's Spirit, but that's only the beginning. The se-cret of renewal is the penetration by the Lord's Spirit into our intel-lect, reason, memory, imagination, will, and then on into our

171

emotions. The psalmist wanted *everything* within him to bless the Lord. Nothing could be excluded or hidden.

An Orchestrated Response

The other evening, my wife and I went to the symphony. We were delighted by the strong leadership of a young conductor. With great vigor he brought all parts of the orchestra into the harmonious crescendo of the theme of the composition.

As I listened and watched, I thought of the psalmist calling for all his inner being to bless the Lord in harmonious unison. All the stringed instruments, horns, and tympani of his varied intellectual, volitional, and emotional faculties were needed. To bring all of our nature into harmony with the soul's desire to bless the Lord is the most demanding prerequisite of consistent renewal.

Growth in spiritual vitality is the result of all our faculties being in tune with the great conductor of the orchestra of our humanity. We bring all that we are into full participation of the music of praise. Yet so often our natures are like a disorderly orchestra playing different scores of music. There is a jangling disharmony within us.

We've all known intellectual Christians whose experience of the gospel converted their reason and intellect but left their emotions untouched; or we've known emotional people who can soar in praise but leave their intellect out of a growing experience with God. We've known Christians who put a great emphasis on service as an expression of an obedient will to bring social change and right wrongs.

Often this action-oriented discipleship grows weak when the resources of spiritual power are left untapped. Activists become exhausted in doing good. The great need for all of us is to have our intellect, emotion, and will completely utilized to bless the Lord in thought and action. Renewal comes when any aspect that has been

172

left out of the orchestration of our faculties to praise the Lord is called into harmony with the rest.

For over thirty years, my ministry has been focused on helping religious church members experience renewal. My experience is that this happens when biblical preaching, inspired by the Holy Spirit, convicts people of their spiritual deadness. People experience renewal differently, but it usually begins when the areas of their life that have been uncommitted to the Lord are brought to Him in full surrender. The probing love of the Lord exposes attitudes, values, practices, and inner tensions that have been kept from Him. Good people are challenged to become great; nice people to become new.

The psalmist had been through a harrowing experience that had given him time to realize how little of his nature was open to the Lord. The Lord invaded his life with sheer grace, so that the psalmist realized that God alone was the source of everything he held crucial and valuable. The possibility of losing his health confronted him with the deep need he had for the Lord. His sense of thanksgiving for the healing he received demanded everything within him to come into harmony with his soul to bless the Lord.

What in your life is reluctant to join in an orchestrated crescendo of praise? Are there memories that need forgiveness and healing? Are there people in your life who need your forgiveness? Are there relationships that need to be surrendered to the Lord's wisdom and guidance? Are there uncommitted areas that have been kept from the Lord? Where in your life are you trying to make it on your own strength? What have you fenced off with a picket line of reservations and resistance to what you know the Lord wants? For what do you find it difficult to praise the Lord?

These inventory questions may help to focus portions of "all" that is within you that are withheld from the Lord's blessing and therefore are not sources of exuberant praise.

When we answer those questions suddenly we realize the place where renewal needs to take place. When we allow the Lord to invade the discordant elements of our nature, we are on the way to a new level of growth—a process that will never end. There will always be something in us that needs to be confessed or surrendered to the Lord. Continuous renewal happens when more and more of our inner self joins with our soul to bless the Lord. When we experience fresh grace in those areas, the Lord's strength will be given.

The Secret of Strength

Thus we come to the promise of having our youth renewed like the eagle's. We need to question what the psalmist meant. A careful study of the eagle reveals that it does not have self-renewing power. What may be meant is the period of plumage when it gets a new set of feathers. Some say that the eagle flies after that with renewed vigor. But I sense that the psalmist was referring to the strength and long life of the eagle and its amazing capacity to soar at great heights. The secret of the eagle's power is not in its wings but in the jet stream in which it is lifted up and is carried to heights it could not attain on its own.

When we bless the Lord with all that is within us, we experience the eagle's strength multiplied by the wind. The symbolism is powerful. Surrender to the infilling and empowering of the Holy Spirit gives us the eagle's capacity to soar in the stream of His limitless power. Our strength is renewed in that it is infused by divine energy. We become capable of thinking beyond our natural ability. Our emotions become released to express love beyond our capacity. The tissues of our bodies are enlivened with supernatural energy.

The result is that our natural energy is no longer drained off in self-effort or fighting against the Lord. Resistance to Him depletes our resources. When we open ourselves in honest vulnerability, we not only are able to use all our natural energies creatively; we also find they are miraculously multiplied by the Spirit's energy in us.

This is the reason some Christians, even in old age, remain vital and exuberant. They have learned the secret of living in the jet stream of the Lord's power. Nothing is hidden. There is no cautious reserve or negative resistance to what the Lord seeks to do in and through them. They have discovered the promise of Isaiah 40:31:

> Those who wait on the LORD
> Shall renew their strength;
> They shall mount up with wings like eagles,
> They shall run and not be weary,
> They shall walk and not faint.

The Source of Renewal

The source of rejuvenated exuberance is that the Lord "satisfies your mouth with good things" (v. 5). What food does for the body, so too the inspiration of the Lord's Spirit does for our inner being. The Lord told Ezekiel to eat the scroll. Symbolically that meant that he was to consume the Word of God. As we mentioned in our consideration of Psalm 1, *meditation* in Hebrew means to chew or ruminate, to digest thoroughly the Word of the Lord. We can give out only so much exuberance as the Lord has rejuvenated within us.

The result is that our youth is renewed. That doesn't mean that we can defy the natural aging process. What it does mean is that we remain young in heart, that the joy of our initial experience of the Lord is constantly renewed, and that we continue to be vigorous in spirit all the days of our life. Remember how you felt when you first trusted the Lord? The freedom, delight, and excitement you knew then is to be multiplied all through the Christian life. The abundance of Christ in us increases as all that is within us is constantly and consistently relinquished to Him.

Many Christians become spiritually old before their time because they lack the spiritual nutrients of prayer, study of the Scriptures, honest, open fellowship with other adventurers, and active ministry to share the Lord's love with those who need Him.

Unless I miss my guess, you and I are on the edge of a new level of growth in the Lord right now. Considering the psalmist's call to bless the Lord with all my being has revealed some reluctant inner portions of my mind and heart. That prompted me to ask, "Can I bless the Lord with all that is within me—all that is within my memory, imagination, will, and vision for the future?"

Even now as I remember His forgiveness, healing, and interventions in the past when I needed Him, I am filled with a new excitement about life in Christ. A new exuberance stirs within me. All the parts of the orchestra of my inner self have been called to bless the Lord. The dark corridors of memory have been illuminated by His love so that I don't need to nurse hidden hurts any longer. My imagination is rejuvenated to consider what I'd be like today were I completely filled with the Lord's Spirit and willing to do what He commands. My vision has been brightened by what the Lord can do with the problems ahead of me today.

As I write this in the early hours of a busy day that will be filled with human impossibilities, suddenly I am alive with expectation for what the Lord is going to do to surprise me with His grace. The psalmist has led me up to the heights, the jet stream of the Lord's Spirit has caught me, and I know this will be an exciting day. I've known far too many days without the jet stream. So I know that the secret of renewal discovered again here in Psalm 103 will have to be rediscovered every day in the future, and the same abandoned praise of blessing the Lord with all that is within me will bring the promised renewal.

We don't have to wait for a renewal conference to mount up with wings like eagles. The Lord waits to bless us right now. All He asks is that we bless Him with all that is within us.

16

Take a Larger Gift
Psalm 116

The woman's voice on the phone was filled with excitement. She could not contain her gratitude for the way the Lord had guided and provided in her life. He had quickened her faith in a wonderful way. She had to give expression of her overflowing heart. The previous Sunday she and her husband had taken a bold step of trusting the Lord, and he had answered their prayers.

Coming Through on a Promise

The occasion was a Missions Sunday. Each year in May our congregation puts a special emphasis on Christ's mission and receives faith promises from our people for above and beyond gifts to mission. That year, in preparation of my message for the day, the Lord had guided me to conclude with a very specific challenge. I asked each member to remember the total income figure he or she had recorded on the previous year's income tax form. Then I urged each person to figure 1 percent of that amount and make that the basis of a faith promise beyond his or her regular tithe.

The idea was that all of us would put that figure down on our faith promise envelope and place it in the offering plate. We were to yield our checkbooks as a vehicle for the transfer of extra funds we would trust the Lord to provide. Our responsibility would be to await expectantly the Lord's provision of the additional amount from some unexpected source and immediately write a check for the amount to the Missions Fund. The monies received would be used to expand our church's outreach of love to the lost and lonely, the hopeless and hungry who desperately need Christ. A list of projects in addition to our regular mission program through the church budget was printed in the bulletin and people could choose the particular project the Lord placed on their hearts.

The woman and her husband had made out their faith promise early in the service prior to my message. When the challenge of the 1 percent was presented, the husband tore up their previous promise and wrote a new one. After the service as they drove home, he and his wife talked about what he had done. The wife said, "I'm so glad! That's what the Lord put on my heart to do, and I am delighted He guided you to the same figure He gave to me." They felt a unity and oneness in the guidance He had inspired in both of them. They expectantly anticipated how He would bless with the extra, unplanned-for income that He would provide. What they did not expect was that the miracle would happen as quickly as it did.

That Sunday evening, the husband tired of the usual round of television programs and announced that he was going to clean off his desk in his study. He is an outstanding radio and television character actor.

Three weeks before, his wife had put a stack of letters on his desk. Since they looked like junk mail, he had never opened them. That evening in order to clean off his desk, he decided to thumb through the stack in preparation for tossing it all into the wastepaper basket. One envelope caught his eye. The return address was obviously from a production company and looked like those that usually contain residual checks for programs done in the past and rerun on radio or television.

He walked out of his study into the living room, where his wife was still watching television. "Why didn't you tell me that stack of junk mail had an envelope from the production company in it?" he asked. Suspecting that the envelope had a check in it, he opened it with excitement. To their amazement, the check inside for residuals was for an amount they had not expected to receive. They quickly calculated the amount in the light of their faith promise. The check was the exact amount of their faith promise, plus the income tax they would have to pay on the income!

The woman's call was one of many letters and phone calls received after that Missions Sunday. Reports of the Lord's provision were astounding. The remarkable result for the whole congregation was the impact of the Lord's willingness to use us to channel His resources to people in need of His grace and material help.

The same thing happened to me. On that Sunday, early in the morning when I was doing my final preparation before going to church, the Lord reminded me that I could not lead my congregation any further than I had dared to go myself. He brought a numerical figure to my mind and gave me the motivation to write a check for the amount to give to the special missions fund in the service. The amount was ten times what I had planned to promise to give.

The Lord didn't want a promise but a check! He assured me that if I wrote the check, He would replenish the amount. Having done that above my regular tithe and giving gave me freedom and gusto as I preached that morning.

The next day I went to a speaking engagement in Washington state. I expected to be paid for my transportation and expenses. Believing in the purposes of the organization to which I spoke, I was delighted to speak as my contribution to its effort. When I finished and was about to leave for the airport to return home, the man in charge of the meeting slipped an envelope into my Bible. Not until I was on the plane, winging my way home, did I open my Bible to study for a message I was to give when I arrived back in Los Angeles. The envelope fell out. When I picked it up and opened it—you guessed it—it was for the full amount of the check I had written the day before.

What happened to me and my people through this adventure of faith invigorated our trust in other areas, where we needed to pray

for what the Lord wanted and wait expectantly for His provision.
The experience confirmed what I have written and spoken so often:
"What the Lord guides, He provides."

A *Psalm of God's Goodness*

The psalmist knew this triumphant promise. In Psalm 116, he
asked himself a question, and answered himself in an astonishing
way.

> What shall I render to the LORD
> For all His benefits toward me?
> I will take up the cup of salvation,
> And call upon the name of the LORD.
> I will pay my vows to the LORD
> Now in the presence of all His people
> (vv. 12–14).

Note the progression. The psalmist asked how he could express
his gratitude to God for all He had done for him, then he answered
himself by saying that he would be open to take a further and larger
gift that God offered. Too, he promised to share the goodness of
God's response with others.

The secret of gallant thanksgiving and praise is to be willing to
receive the larger gift. "What shall I render? I will take!" The
psalmist had found the lavishly generous heart of God and had
discovered that the finest way to bless Him is to accept more of what
He has available and ready to provide. There is no *quid pro quo* of
drudgery here, no bartered obedience for blessings. Instead, gratitude had produced the attitude of receptivity to accept more from
the open hand of God.

We are often told that the Lord loves a cheerful giver. The statement is true and has implications not only for our tithes and offerings, but for our willingness to share our faith, care for people, and

give ourselves away unstintingly in all of life. Still, the psalm presses us on. We cannot give away what we do not have. Therefore, the Lord wants to give us more of His love, His Spirit's power, and His providential care so we can have more to give away. What He puts in, He wants us to give out. Our problem is that often we are reluctant receivers.

God longs to bless us. He does not say, "This I have given you and there will be no more until you measure up to my standards." Instead, He lovingly says, "All this I have offered and given freely, but you have barely tasted My goodness. Now go on, take a larger gift. Drink fully from the cup of salvation and drain it dry; then look into the cup and you will be amazed that I have filled it up again. The cup of My salvation is artesian. It will always be full, however much you drink from it. Call on Me for more than you ever realized was available."

The Lord takes delight in getting us beyond our own resources so that we have no sure means of support other than in Him. He honors those who accept what He gives and go on to receive more. The question that lingers on our minds, therefore, is why we remain spiritual paupers when He has opened the treasure of His heart and said, "Here, take what is yours!"

The Cup of Salvation

What is the larger gift? The psalmist said it was the cup of salvation (v. 13). Both words, *cup* and *salvation*, are drenched with propitious meaning in the Bible.

The cup meant more than a drinking vessel to the Hebrews. Figuratively, it meant one's lot or experience. Both joyous and sorrowful experiences are implied, as we see here in Psalm 116—*the cup of salvation*—or conversely in Psalm 11:6, "Upon the wicked He will rain coals,/Fire and brimstone and a burning wind;/This shall be the portion of their *cup*" (italics added).

The cup as blessing is stressed in Psalm 16:5–6, where the Lord Himself is the desire of the psalmist's heart:

> You, O LORD, are the portion of my
>   inheritance and my *cup*;
> You maintain my lot.
> The lines have fallen to me in pleasant places;
> Yes, I have a good inheritance.

The idea behind such praise is that when the Lord portioned out the land to the tribes of Israel, the priests were given a far greater gift than land; their inheritance was to know and serve the Lord.

As we have noted in Psalm 23:5, the word *cup* is also synonymous with our hearts or our life: "My cup overflows." In Psalm 75:8–9, the metaphor is mixed. The *cup* here contains blessing for those who drink of the rich, red wine of God's goodness, but the dregs are left for the reluctant who wait, resisting God's best:

> For in the hand of the LORD there is a cup,
> And the wine is red;
> It is fully mixed, and He pours it out;
> Surely its dregs shall all the wicked of the earth
> Drain and drink down.
> But I will declare forever,
> I will sing praises to the God of Jacob.

These references establish the meaning of the *cup* as our inherited gift from the Lord and our experience of it in daily life.

The cup takes on deeper significance in the New Testament, as its meaning unfolds. Jesus spoke of His cup as His destiny to save the world from sin on the cross.

When James and John came to Him saying, "Teacher, we want You to do for us whatever we ask," He responded, "What do you want Me to do for you?" Their request was narrow and selfish. "Grant us that we may sit, one on Your right hand and the other on

Your left, in Your glory." Jesus' response was to tell them that they didn't know what they were asking. Then He asked, "Can you drink the cup that I drink, and be baptized with the baptism that I am baptized with?" The Master pressed them into a deeper understanding of His *cup*. "Even the Son of Man did not come to be served, but to serve, and to give His life a ransom for many" (Mark 11:35–45).

In Gethsemane, Jesus knew His cup was the suffering of the cross when He prayed. He acknowledged the anguish ahead and accepted anew the purpose of His incarnation. "'Father, if it is Your will, remove this cup from Me nevertheless not My will, but Yours, be done'" (John 22:42). He took His cup of suffering for our sins so that He could fill our cup with the blessings of forgiveness, reconciliation, and eternal life.

Later, when the disciples looked back on the cross and remembered the Lord's call to become great by being a servant, they too realized that their cup meant a cross of death to self. They were able to face that awesome challenge because of another cup, the cup of the new covenant in Christ's blood. Each time they broke bread and drank of the cup in remembrance of the Last Supper and Christ's death and resurrection, they were given courage to ask for a much larger gift than self-aggrandizement. They received the greatest gift of all—Christ's indwelling presence and power. Their cup was their calling, and Christ's cup to them was unlimited spiritual strength to accomplish that calling to His glory and not their own.

The apostle Paul was able to blend the rich heritage of the Hebrew meaning of the cup and Christ' cup of new life. Surely he had Psalm 116 on his mind when he wrote of the cup of blessing and identified it with the communion with Christ and all that He offers. "The cup of blessing which we bless, is it not the communion of the blood of Christ? . . ." (1 Cor. 10:16). Through the shedding of Christ's blood, a covenant of grace had been established, the atonement was given, and Christ Himself became the cup of salvation.

What does that mean for us when we ask with the psalmist,

"What shall I render to the Lord for all His benefits?" Sublimely this: The larger gift beyond all that we can ask is to receive the infilling of Christ's Spirit. With Him all else we would ask is made possible.

Total Salvation

That realization leads us to the word *salvation*. The cup of salvation, nothing less, is what gratitude for his past blessings had prompted the psalmist to take with boldness. As we have noted, *salvation* in the psalms means deliverance from danger as well as protection, provision, and blessing. As Christians, our understanding goes way beyond that.

In the cup of blessing Christ offers us, *salvation* means both being saved *from* and saved *for*. We are delivered from sin, evil, and the power of death, for our abundant life now and eternal life forever. In the New Testament, salvation, *sōtēria*, means wholeness, healing, and health. Through Christ our brokenness is replaced with wholeness of mind, will, and emotion around the dynamic center of Christ's indwelling, integrating Spirit. Our memories are healed, our emotional hurts are washed clean of the pus of rejection and disappointment, and our hearts are filled with authentic love for ourselves and others.

The very tissues of our bodies are invaded by the Great Physician. Our personalities are progressively transformed to be like Him. Fear of death is gone. We are filled with the resiliency of Christ's resurrection—and our own—each day, and on that day when we will graduate into the next phase of our eternal life in heaven. Such is the cup of salvation we are able to drink—and there are no dregs at the bottom.

In that context, we come to drink each day, hourly, during our pilgrimage on earth. When we drink the salvation of Christ's cup, we are given the key to facing our challenges and troubles. Our task is to listen in prayer until we know the particular gift He offers for our perplexities, then we can ask for what He is graciously waiting to give.

Every difficulty is an unclaimed territory in which the Lord has a plan and a purpose. He wants to bless us with exactly what we need to do His will. When we ask Him, He reveals what He wants to give to each person or circumstance that troubles us. He will show us what we are to be and do, what He offers to make it possible, and how He will accomplish it through us.

> The living Christ is surely here
> To set us free from crippling fear
> When we receive His healing touch
> We never can expect too much. [1]

Co-workers with God

Drinking fully of the cup of salvation each day clarifies what the Lord offers to do and gives us motivating power for what we are to do to cooperate as partners with Him in His blessing. That's what the psalmist meant when he committed himself to pay his vows in the presence of all the Lord's people. For him that meant worship in the temple, the offering of sacrifices, and the giving of his tithes and offerings.

For us, all those practices are implied, but also much more. When prayer defines what we are to do and what the Lord will provide to make it possible, we must act as if the blessing has been realized. We can thank the Lord in advance that what He gave us the courage to envision, the boldness to ask for, and the confidence to expect, will be done by Him in His way and in His timing. We ask once and thank Him thousands of times as we wait for the fulfillment of the vision He has given. Often our trust must be expressed in a step of faith that makes us participants with the Lord in the unfolding of His will.

When the Israelites crossed the Jordan into the promised land of

Canaan, the priests carrying the Ark of the Covenant had to put their feet into the Jordan before the Lord rolled back the water and made a passageway possible. The same is true for us. We must act on the Lord's guidance, claim His promises, and then He gives a greater blessing.

That's what happened to the couple who put their feet in the water by making a faith promise. The venture was concern for Christ's mission, but they had to sign the promise. The Lord did the rest. The only thing they were required to do after that was deposit the check in their checking account and write their check to the Missions Fund. They paid their vow, the congregation of the Lord's people were encouraged by the account of how He had worked, and the missions project they designated was blessed.

The same principle is applicable to all of life. What is the specific gift the Lord wants to give? Gratitude for what He's done previously gives us the courage to ask for it. Most of us ask far too little because our vision is far too small. When we allow the Lord to bless us, we are quickened in our willingness to ask for more. The Lord wants to have us drink deeply from the cup of salvation because that alone will satisfy our personal needs. When we are healed by His Spirit, we will want to turn our prayers to the needs of people around us and the situations that need His grace. To drink consistently from the cup of salvation creates the desire to offer it to a world parched for the only One who quenches thirsty souls.

In a way, our thirst for the Spirit is never quenched. Each new day creates a fresh thirst to be slaked. That leads us full circle to where we ended the previous chapter. Christ Himself is the cup of salvation. Within us He releases the flow of living water. He promised, "He who believes in Me, as the Scripture has said, out of his heart will flow rivers of living waters'" (John 7:38). The flow is unlimited because His resources are undiminishable.

Following that image, you and I are meant to be the cup from which others have their first taste of His Spirit. To extend the metaphor, that's really our cup—our awesome calling and destiny!

17

Let God Help You!
Psalm 121

At every stage of life we face perplexities and problems. The journey of our life seems waylaid by potential difficulties. We cast about for help from people, ourselves, and then, finally, from God. When at last we come to God with the need, His response is usually, "Why did you wait so long to ask for help?"

One of the most disturbing observations I have made about myself and so many others with whom I have talked in depth about needs in their lives, is that there often is a time lag between when we become aware of a problem and when we finally allow God to help us.

The Four Looks

We usually go through the process of what I call the four looks: the outward look to others for help, the inward look to muster our own abilities, the upward look to God when others and we cannot help ourselves sufficiently, and then the forward look to the future, utilizing what the Lord has given us to help us. My prayer is that I would move to the last two looks more quickly—or even better, to look immediately to God for help.

The other day, a woman in my church shared what she perceived to be an overwhelming problem. She was done in, tired out, and uptight in meeting her family's needs. "Why not let God help you?" I asked.

"That's a strange way of putting it," she responded. "Do you mean I have a choice?"

"Yes!" I asserted with urgency. "You have a decision to make: Are you going to manage this problem on your own or cry out to God for help?"

The woman was shocked. "You're suggesting that I may be blocking God's efforts to help me. I've tried everything and everybody else. How do I 'let God help me'?"

I tried to share what I've learned over the years about how to surrender my needs to the Lord more quickly and how to allow Him to help me. I told her honestly about my strong will and my determined desire to be self-sufficient.

"When I let go of my own tenacious control of problematic people and situations, I lower the barrier I so often erect around my mind and heart," I confided. "He's never failed to give me supernatural power in response to a prayer of complete surrender. He helps me to see deeply into the problem with wisdom; He gives me discernment to know what to do; and He provides faith, courage, and endurance to follow through. I am amazed at how He steps in to change people and the circumstances that brought me at last to look to Him for help. He is faithful. Sometimes He changes the situation, but He always changes my attitude toward it. If I've made any progress in the Christian life, it is in not waiting so long before I cry out for help."

At the end of our conversation, the woman gave the Lord her problem and asked for help. He stepped in, first to give her strength and then to enable her to trust Him with her husband and children. She had been playing God in her efforts to be all things to all of them. Because she had not yielded the control of her own life to the Lord, she had held an imperious control over the people she loved. Now when problems arise she does not blame others or seek solutions from them. She turns first to the Lord. Her will is ready to allow Him to help her.

A *Psalm of Direction*

In Psalm 121, the psalmist faced danger. He was either on a pilgrimage or a journey. A range of hills or mountains lay ahead. In them would be robbers, wolves, and treacherous passages in which he could slip and fall. In the valley he knew there was no other way than through the hills to his destination. How would he make it? The perplexity led him into a dialogue with his own inner being. He took the four looks I mentioned earlier. Note the progression.

Looking Out

"I will lift up my eyes to the hills—" (v. 1). That's the outward look at his problems. So often interpretation of this psalm has suggested that the hills were a source of help to the psalmist. The more I study the psalm, I am convinced that the hills were looked to for help and rejected as a source of strength in danger.

Surely we've all had times in the mountains when we were inspired by lofty peaks that pierced the sky. The majesty and the grandeur lifted us out of ourselves to think about eternal things. But what if we had to cross the mountains on foot? What if, from a distance, we had to contemplate the possible perils they contained? Looking to the hills doesn't give us strength. They accurately focus the problems over which we must climb.

When we shift the metaphor, looking to the hills can be understood as our outward look for help from people or groups. "Somebody help me!" we cry out. If the response is slow in coming or complete silence, we are tempted to feel no one cares. The despair leads us to ask the crucial question the psalmist asked in his inward look.

"From whence comes my help?" Note the New King James Version punctuation, which corrects the inadequate translation of the

189

King James Version. It is in keeping with the best Hebrew language scholarship that interprets the clause as an interrogative and not as a completion of a statement. The King James Version implies that the hills are the source of the help.

The basis of that rendering is that the psalmist had the hills of Jerusalem in mind—Mount Zion and Mount Moriah—both metaphors of Yahweh's might. The more accurate translation is to read: "I will lift up my eyes to the hills (pause) From whence comes my help?" Two looks are implied: a look to the hills for help and then an inward look for some self-help remedy—which leads to the real question, as to the ultimate reliability of our own courage and strength.

Looking In

We live in a time when the inward look is stressed as the source of our sufficiency. Self-esteem is touted as the cure-all. We are to believe in ourselves, become self-reliant, and love ourselves. I'm for self-esteem, if it is rooted in the Lord's accepting love for us and in His Spirit as the source of our courage and boldness.

The truth of the matter is that many of us look inward to ourselves for answers to our problems and are disappointed. We don't have the insight or resourcefulness to solve life's problems, so we become worried and filled with anxiety. We muddle through the midst of problems trying desperately to work out some solution. We become exhausted and totally disappointed.

The psalmist's inward look resulted in the pertinent question, "Just where can I go to find help?" The dialogue with his own soul produced an answer, one he had known all along but came to only after he had tried other sources of help. In despair, he finally lifted his eyes in prayer to the ultimate source of help. That prompted his admonition of assurance to his own soul.

"My help comes from the LORD,/Who made heaven and earth" (v. 2). The One who made us sustains us. He knows and cares about us and is ready to help us in the ups and downs of life. Just as He is the creator, He is the recreator of the person He wants us to become through what we experience. The psalm stresses the sovereignty of God over all our affairs.

We cannot breathe a breath or think a thought without Him; yet He has created us with a free will so we can choose to love Him and call on Him in times of need. Knowing that our help comes from Him and crying out for His help is an expression of maturity. Immaturity is thinking we can make it on our own.

Looking Ahead

Throughout the rest of the psalm, the psalmist stressed three reasons why the Lord is a reliable aid in our difficulties for the rest of our lives: He always watches over us, He is at our side to strengthen us, and He brings the maximum growth out of all we will ever go through—now and in the future. Let's consider each of these truths.

1. *God's Providential Care.* "He who keeps Israel/Shall neither slumber nor sleep" (v. 4) tells us that He is at work night and day interceding, arranging blessings, and influencing our thoughts.

Bishop Quayle, a leader of the Methodist church years ago, related an experience of the Lord's persistent providence. One night he worked into the early morning hours trying to finish his work and solve problems. The Bible on his desk was open to Psalm 121. At a moment of intense pressure Quayle's eye fell on the assurance of the Lord's twenty-four-hour vigil of watchful care. He was reminded that his efforts to work for God rather than allowing God to work through him were defeating and extremely exhausting. In his inner being he heard the Lord say, "Quayle, there's no need for both of us to stay up all night. I'm going to stay up anyway. You go to bed and get a good sleep."

The psalmist could go to sleep under the stars knowing that the Lord would watch over him. No harm would come to him. How often we need to be reminded of this truth when sleep refuses to bless our tired minds and bodies or when we are awakened in the middle of the night by unresolved tensions. We toss and turn, fretting over the anxieties with which we went to bed.

One evening I spoke at a meeting of an adult group of my church. The meeting was held in the home of dear friends. To express a warm welcome to their pastor, they kept a place open in their driveway for my car. A beautiful, gothic-lettered sign read, "Please reserve for Dr. Ogilvie."

After my talk and a time of prayer with the group, my host and I walked out to my car. "Why not take the sign with you? You may need it," he said warmly. I thanked him and put the sign in the front seat of my car.

The next morning when I left home early for a breakfast meeting, I found it there waiting for me. A humorous idea popped into my mind. My wife, Mary Jane, was still asleep. I crept back into the house, went to our bedroom, and without waking her, put the sign and the stand in my place in our king-sized bed. When she made the bed after her breakfast, she found the sign and called me at my office with laughter in her voice. She had some nice, affectionate things to say about the fact that she was glad that place in our bed was reserved for me.

Later, after a night in which I found it difficult to sleep because of some concerns, Mary Jane added eight words to the sign and put it in the bed while I showered the next morning. When I returned to the bedroom there it was: "Reserved for Dr. Ogilvie *to sleep trusting the One who never sleeps!*"

I got the point! I had taken over the Lord's job description. I was doing His work when I should have been sleeping in preparation for a new day. I would need to be rejuvenated to tackle the concerns with His help.

Some time ago I was part of a group of Christian leaders gathered to solve a perplexing problem. We set aside two days at a retreat center to talk and pray through a solution. By the end of the first day we were deadlocked in conflict over what should be done. All the alternatives seemed equally unsatisfactory to win unanimous approval. Late at night we were all bleary and exhausted.

An elder statesman who is a seasoned saint offered a suggestion. "Let's go to bed, trust this whole thing to the Lord, ask Him to work in our minds while we sleep, and come together after breakfast to see if we can allow Him to break the bind we're in. Let's allow the unslumbering Lord and sleepless Helper to take care of this while we get some rest."

You guessed it! The next morning we all gave up our determination to sway the group with our plan and all began to seek the mind of the Lord for His plan. What evolved was so much better than any of our proposals, we were astounded.

The psalmist knew that the Lord would guide his steps through the treacherous passages of the mountain terrain the next day. He could sleep in peace with the assurance that He would make his steps decisive and secure. The words "He will not allow your foot to be moved" (v. 3) mean that He will keep us from slipping. A wrong step would have plummeted the psalmist to his death.

The implication for us is that the One who neither slumbers nor sleeps lets us do both serenely, so that the following day we can allow Him to guide our steps. How does the Lord help us? He is ever-ready to give us clarity about the next step in His strategy for us, but again, we must want His help. A decision must be made. We have been given the freedom to accept or reject His direction in our choices and decisions, and He also wants to help implement what He has instigated in our mind.

2. *God's Protective Care.* This leads to the second way the Lord helps us.

> The LORD is your keeper;
> The LORD is your shade at your right hand.
> The sun shall not strike you by day,
> Nor the moon by night (vv. 5–6).

The word *keep* means protection, reminding us of the way the shepherd cares for his sheep. The metaphor in this psalm is expanded by the idea that the Lord not only watches over us but is at our right hand. The protector of a king or some leader always stood at his right hand. He was there to ward off attacks and to hold the armor and weapons ready in battle.

That's what Christ, God with us, does for us. He stood by our side in the incarnation and promised to be with us always (see Matt. 28:20). We are never alone.

We do not need to ask Him to be with us. He promised that and is faithful to His word. He is the "Keeper." Our Lord guards us, intercedes for us, pleads our case, and equips us for life's battles.

"The sun shall not strike you by day,/Nor the moon by night" (v. 6). The danger of sun- or moon-stroke was very real in the psalmist's mind in the context of the understanding of his time. Sunstroke was a constant peril of the traveler in Palestine, and there was a mysterious belief that the moon affected a person's mental stability. Our word *lunacy* (Latin *luna*, "moon") comes from that. The idea was that there was a correlation between the moon's phases and mental and emotional disturbance.

The import of this for us is simply that nothing or no one, day or night, sleeping or awaking, can ultimately harm us. The Lord may not keep us from trouble, but we can be sure He will be with us in it and use it for our growth in greatness.

3. *God's Preserving Care.* We've seen how the Lord providentially watches over us and how He protects us. Now the psalm presses on to consider how He *preserves* us. The word seems out of sync with our contemporary usage.

How does the Lord preserve us? The word means to maintain, conserve, and keep from destruction. The most crucial ministry of Christ present with us is not just beside us, but within us. Jesus promised that He would abide in us (see John 15:4). His preservation of us is from within. He takes on the responsibility of making us like Himself, guiding our thoughts, giving us His attitudes, and enabling us to love, forgive, care and minister by His power.

The psalmist claimed the preservation of the soul against all evil in our "going out and coming in." Those words encompass all of life when we begin a day and end it and all happens in between. Just as the Lord does not slumber while we sleep, He never forgets nor forsakes us in all the demands and difficulties of any day.

We wonder if the psalmist had Deuteronomy 28:6 on his mind when he claimed the Lord's daytime care: "Blessed shall you be when you come in, and blessed shall you be when you go out." Those words, along with Deuteronomy 6:4–9 were repeated by every Hebrew as he or she touched the *mezuza* attached to the door frame of his or her house. "The LORD our God, the LORD is one!" He would preserve His people in their coming and going.

Although the language reflects another era, F. B. Meyer's personal witness of the impact of Psalm 121 sparkles with zest:

O unslumbering Keeper! O sleepless watcher Shade from the heat, shelter from the cold, protector from assault, transformer of ill to good, escort when we go out, home when we return! Thou art the complement of our need. We are content to suffer the loss of all things, to find all in Thee. And therefore we betake ourselves to thy shadow till life's calamities are overpast. [1]

Psalm 121 has shown us how to let God help us. He is our power, protector, and preservation. Our challenge is to trust Him for rest at night and resiliency during the day. The great need is to turn our difficulties over to Him for guidance and help as soon as they confront us, not after we have struggled to solve them by ourselves and failed. He is ready to help now!

18

God Is There to Meet You
Psalm 139

Mary Crowley of Dallas, Texas, is one of America's leading Christian businesswomen. She is the president of Home Interiors and Gifts, Inc., a multimillion dollar hostess plan, direct sales corporation.

In the past twenty-five years her company has grown from a small business she started in her garage to a successful enterprise that grossed over four hundred million dollars last year. With complete trust in the Lord and unbounded enthusiasm for life as His gift, she has recruited and trained thirty-nine thousand women as her sales representatives throughout the United States.

Recently, Mary was in Los Angeles to speak to the Mayor's Prayer Breakfast. I had the delight of introducing this adventuresome disciple of our Lord. In preparation for that, we had a time together that made an indelible impression on me. I wanted to know the secret of her success and her vibrant, positive approach to life. What I learned was that she has trusted the Lord each step of the way for His unfolding strategy for her life. She believes that success is doing what He wants her to do and doing it with a commitment to excellence. Two purposes undergird all she does: to honor God and to bless and serve people. These goals have been expressed in consistent tithing of every dollar she makes and in caring for the thousands of people who work for her.

I have seldom met a person who has greater hope and confidence in the future. Why? Her response is, "Do not be afraid of tomorrow. God is already there!"

A *Psalm of God's Accessibility*

Such is the liberating conviction to which the psalmist came in Psalm 139. A time of difficulty and false accusations by people had driven him to a profound time of prayer. In communion with God, he discovered two powerful aspects of God's nature—His omniscience and His omnipresence. The Lord knew all about him, and there was no place he could go where the Lord was not there to meet him.

So often the interpretation of this psalm has stressed the inescapable presence of God. We are reminded that we cannot flee from Him, that He is like Frances Thompson's *Hound of Heaven*, tracking us until we stop running and accept His sovereignty over us. This emphasis in the exposition of the psalm empathizes with the efforts we've all made to escape both God's judgment and His love. We've all known times, both before and after we became Christians, when we thought and acted like people who were seeking to flee from the Lord's seeing and knowing eye.

However, there's a positive side to the psalm which is too often neglected. The fact that the Lord knows all and is everywhere is the basis of a viable hopefulness for the future. Wherever we go, whomever we meet, the Lord is already there waiting for us. He not only comes to us in times of need and gives us supernatural power for life's difficulties and challenges, He also goes before us to prepare the way.

Almost every day, I talk to people who are worried about the future. Their tomorrows are filled with uncertainties. What's going to happen? What will people do? How will problems be resolved? How will the next steps be revealed? These questions put a cloud over our tomorrows and fill our todays with anxiety.

We cannot be free to enjoy life until we discover that the Lord has dealt forgivingly with our yesterdays and is way out ahead of us preparing opportunities, opening doors, conditioning the thoughts and reactions of people, and arranging His best for us.

Our task is to dare to move forward under His guidance, expectantly anticipating what He has graciously drafted in His building plan for our lives. I find that idea to be both very exciting and a source of deep inner peace. To realize that confidence, we must experience the progressive steps through which the psalmist went in arriving at a profound trust in the prevenient Lord of the future.

We must begin where the psalmist began or we will miss the message of this psalm. He is gripped with the conviction that God knows him better than he knows himself.

> O LORD, You have searched me and known me.
> You know my sitting down and my rising up;
> You understand my thought afar off.
> You comprehend my path and my lying down,
> And are acquainted with all my ways
> (vv. 1–3).

God Knows It All!

The firm conviction of God's omniscience, that He knows everything, relieves us of the burden of thinking that we are on our own with the responsibility of developing our lives to the best of our meager abilities. We develop the idea that life is a struggle, in which prayer is an effort to get God's attention and then convince Him to help us. Our strenuous religion becomes one of trying to involve God in our needs and opportunities. We think of Him as aloof, uninvolved, and One who will help us if we word our prayers correctly and live a life worthy of His concern. He is envisaged as a famous consultant whom we seek to call in to help us.

The other day, a friend of mine and I were talking about a crucial project in which we are involved. The work is a strategic ministry, and its future development is beyond our wisdom. We had decided what we should do but admitted we did not have the skills to pull it off. "What we need to do is call in the best consultant in America to help us," my friend advised. When we agreed on who that was we wondered if we could get on his schedule, whether we could afford his time, and whether he would consider our needs worthy of his involvement.

Reflecting on that incident, I realized that often we think of God in the same way. We forget that He's in charge of our lives, and we are employed by Him rather than He by us! We can't call God into any area; He is there before we get there.

He Knows Our Thoughts

The psalmist went deeper in that realization. God knows our thoughts even before we clothe them with words. The fact that He knows our thoughts is a reminder that He can and does help form them. As the author of thought, He engenders the content of our prayers so that we can pray for what He is more ready to give than we may have been to ask.

Knowing that, we can join the psalmist in praise.

> For there is not a word on my tongue,
> But behold, O LORD, You know it altogether.
> You have hedged me behind and before,
> And laid Your hand upon me.
> Such knowledge is too wonderful for me;
> It is high, I cannot attain it (vv. 4–6).

What cannot be attained by human effort is given as a gift of love. The Lord who knows all about us, even our inner thoughts, invades our minds to assure us that He can guide our direction and be there waiting for us when we arrive. The joyous realization of His omniscience has freed us to rediscover the powerful truth of His omnipresence—not only where we are now, but where we are going in the future.

He Knows Our Whereabouts

The thought of fleeing God turns into an expectation of finding Him in the situations and people ahead of us. The psalmist reviewed the illusions of where he might go where God was not, only to realize He is never absent in any place or circumstance. "Where can I go from Your Spirit?/Or where can I flee from Your presence?" he asked (v. 7). Heaven, hell, the horizon with the wings of the morning, the depth of the sea, day or night? The Lord is already there. The words *You are there* in the Hebrew are literally *There—Thou!* Such truth does not frighten us as much as it frees us of the fear of the future.

The Lord has made us for Himself to love, serve, and glorify Him. That was the next thought that gripped the psalmist's God-invaded mind.

> I will praise You, for I am fearfully
> and wonderfully made
> Marvelous are Your works,
> And that my soul knows very well (v. 14).

He went on to claim that the Lord knew him before he was born and had worked out his destiny. With awe and wonder he considered that gripping truth.

> Your eyes saw my substance, being yet unformed.
> And in Your book they all were written,
> The days fashioned for me,
> When as yet there were none of them.
> How precious also are Your thoughts to me, O God!
> How great is the sum of them!

If I should count them, they would be
  more in number than the sand;
When I awake, I am still with You (vv. 16–18).

The Implications for Us

What does this mean for you and me? Everything! The Lord has a purpose and plan for each of us, a personal, particularized destiny. He has a will for each of us which is unique and special, envisioned for no one else. His ultimate will for everyone is that we should experience His love and accept our status as His beloved daughters and sons. Within that eternal status, He has a plan for each of us to enjoy the abundant life filled with His presence and power for living out what He has ordained to be His individualized strategy. To help us accomplish that, He guides us in the direction we should go and is always before us to maximize each relationship and opportunity.

During the preparation and writing of this chapter, I talked to a young executive in my congregation who was concerned about his future. He was restless to get on with his career. Filled with the normal ambition of a dynamic professional in his late twenties, he wanted to be sure of his next steps. He had not considered that God had a plan for him. "How can I find that?" he asked.

We talked about having a converted "wanter." That captured his brilliant mind. Wanting what God wanted for him had not been a part of his thinking. Though he was a Christian, he had felt that sorting out his professional plans was his job. Yet when we discussed how much of his time and energy was spent at work, he agreed that God would want to help him discover His will for what was actually shaping his values and destiny.

We prayed together that the Lord would guide His wanting and prepare the way before him, then we talked out what he wanted to do with his life as God's person. What steps would bring him closer to that life goal? Any new position would have to meet that qualification. When he accepted that the Lord had gone ahead to prepare his way, he was able to relax and enjoy where he was presently. He surrendered His wanting to be an instrument for the revelation of the Lord's will.

A few weeks later, a job opportunity opened up that was tailor-made for him as a perfect next step. To his amazement, he learned that the decision to offer him that position had been made at the very time he was wrestling with his future. The Lord had prepared him for what He had prepared.

In very different circumstances, a woman discovered the same assurance about the prevenient providence of God. She faced a seemingly insolvable problem at work. She was deadlocked with a fellow worker in conflict that had resulted in strained communication during the day and anxious, sleepless nights. As a confrontation drew near, she came to me to talk out what she was to do.

We talked much about the woman who had become her enemy and threatening foe. What had made her the way she was? What were the dynamics causing the competitive conflict between them? Could we dare to believe that God wanted reconciliation, the resolution of the conflict, and a mutually affirming friendship between them?

We both agreed that He did, then I asked, "Do you believe that the same Lord who is here with us is also with this woman, and is preparing her for this forthcoming confrontation?" She had not thought of that. The lines of worry on her face seemed to soften as she considered the possibility.

I said, "The Lord loves this person as much as He does you. He is at work right now breaking down the walls of hostility and resistance. When you meet with her, He will have her ready!" We entered into a time of prayer for her, asking God to change both of them so that His plan for their working relationship could be accomplished.

A few days later when my friend met with the woman she found her amazingly receptive. She confided to my friend, "The other day when I was thinking about you and nursing all my grievances about you, suddenly a thought hit me. 'Why am I so hard on her? What insecurity is causing me to fear her? We both have gifts and we ought to help each other.'"

The Lord had softened her hatred. He had opened the way for their reconciliation and engendered the friendship that resulted. He was there before, during, and after the meeting for which my friend had prayed, claiming that the Lord would go before her to prepare the way.

Facing the Realities

I wish I could say that Psalm 139 ended as well. Instead, the psalmist did not follow to its triumphant conclusion his own discovery about God. He used God's providence over his life as a basis of justifying his hate for his enemies. He was even more determined to hate those who hated the Lord. His feeling of the Lord's vindication of his life made him vindictive rather than victorious with forgiving love.

This honest expression at the end of so powerful a realization of God's care helps us grapple with reality. Many of us have experienced grace and still have little viable faith that God will invade our impossibilities with intervening help. Surely that's why so many Christians miss what the Lord has gone ahead of them to prepare. Elizabeth Barrett Browning flatly stated that sad truth.

> Earth's crammed with Heaven,
> And every common bush afire with God,
> But only he who sees takes off his shoes.[1]

Many of us stand blind to the unlimited possibilities, refusing to take off our shoes in reverence for what the Lord has waiting for us. I've discovered that living expectantly sensitizes us to anticipate and to enjoy what the Lord has been getting ready for us in people, situations, and circumstances. He *is* there waiting for us, and coupled with the gift of the prepared blessings, He wants to give eyes of faith to discern what He's done. He would have that discovery build a confident faith in His ability to plan our future and be there to maximize it. Only then can we sing William Cowper's words with new gusto.

> Ye fearful saints fresh courage take,
> The clouds ye so much dread
> Are big with mercy, and shall break
> In blessings on your head.

19

Falling Into Greatness
Psalm 145

A friend of mine, a high flier in the circus in his youth, tells me that the secret of becoming a successful trapeze artist is in overcoming the fear of falling.

"Once you know that the net below will catch you, you stop worrying about falling," he says. "You actually learn to fall successfully! What I mean is, you can concentrate on catching the trapeze swinging toward you and not on falling because repeated falls in the past have convinced you that the net is strong and reliable when you do fall. The rope in the net hurts only if you stiffen up and resist it. The result of falling and being caught by the net is a mysterious confidence and daring on the trapeze. You fall less. Each fall makes you able to risk more!"

Learning from Failure

The same is true of life. I know—I've fallen often. Who hasn't? The Lord is like that net. He catches me when I fall, and when I am caught by His everlasting arms, I discover His true greatness. He is the forgiving Lord whose love never fails. If I had never fallen in the failures of my life, I would never have known the absolute reliability of His grace. He is always there when I fail. The more sure I am of that, the less I fear failure, and amazingly, the less I fail! I am learning how to fall into greatness.

Falling into greatness? The words seem contradictory, but only at first. Allow me to explain. What I've learned about falling successfully is that in times of inadequacy, I experience how great the Lord is. In times of ease or triumph I can readily acknowledge His glory with gratitude; but when life goes bump, I realize the greatness of His gracious heart.

There are aspects of the Lord's nature we never experience until we are forced to face our inadequacy, insufficiency, and inability. We trip and fall in our mistakes, poor decisions, or when we experience a breakdown in communication with people we love. Sometimes we stumble in our careers or in accomplishing our goals. There are those times when we deny what we believe by the way we act, or we do the one thing we'd promised ourselves we'd never do. With 20/20 hindsight we look back and hurt over what we said or did. Some temptation to pride or an infraction of what's right has rapped on our door, and we've given in to what we knew was wrong or was less than maximum for us.

Often our falls occur in the areas where we have attested the greatest convictions and strength. We boldly talk about these areas, and then we are confronted by the inconsistency between our words and deeds. We realize what hypocrites we are. Dreams are smashed or fondest hopes fade. We are forced to give up our image of superior spirituality and realize that we're no different from others who struggle with the ambiguities and difficulties of life and know human failures.

By far the most painful falls are in our relationship with the Lord Himself. We tell Him we love Him and yet deny Him total access to our minds and hearts. We fall out of deep fellowship with Him. Prayer becomes a duty and serving Him an arduous obligation. The closeness we once felt with Him is lost. When life falls apart in some area, we cry out for help and the cry sticks like a bone in our throat. We wonder what right we have to ask for help when we have turned our backs on Him so often. Can His love reach out to people like us?

The Ever-present Net

At that point, we fall into greatness—the Lord's and the possibility of our own through Him. We are astounded by the indefatigable love He has for us. Our falls can't change His faithfulness. That greatness engenders a new freedom in the future. We become people who can risk doing His will, knowing that when we fall He will catch us, put us back on our feet, and give us a new beginning.

That greatness is expressed in compassionate, accepting love for others who fall. Spiritual arrogance is swept away, replaced by empathy for the fallible nature we share. We become partners with the Lord in catching people who fall in their mistakes, failures, and sins. The truly great Christians I know have passed through some experience of their own insufficiency and impotence, and through the fall have been given the precious gift of humility and tender love for others.

A Psalm of Liberation

Such is the liberating message of Psalm 145, a song of praise for the greatness of God. At first, the psalmist extolled Him for that greatness in creation, His mighty acts goodness, and righteousness; then suddenly the song of praise shifts from what God does to what He is.

With awe and wonder, the psalmist shared his own experience.

> The LORD is gracious and full of compassion,
> Slow to anger and great in mercy.
> The LORD is good to all,
> And His tender mercies are over all His works (vv. 8–9).

How did the psalmist know about this depth of God's love? From his own life and careful observation of others, he had learned that "The LORD upholds all who fall,/And raises up all those who are bowed down" (v. 14).

In Hebrew, *upholds* is a predicate explaining the nature of the Lord. His name here is *The Lord upholds*. He supports those who fall in the walk of life. The metaphor shifts to affirm that He also raises up those who are bowed down. The image is of a reed bent down under the heat of the sun or the blasts of the wind.

We *fall* because of what we do with life; we are *bowed down* because of what life does to us. We either fall down or are pushed down. In either case the Lord is there to help us with love we never imagined was possible.

I am convinced that what the psalmist knew about the greatness of God's grace had been learned in the difficulties of falling in his own life, and in the life of Israel as the people of God. He could praise God for His compassion and mercy because he had fallen into the strong arms of greatness in times of failure.

Personally Loved

The psalm is attributed to David and is the last in the Psalter that bears his name. It expresses the most profound discovery David made about the mercy of God in the midst of his anguish over his sin. What is crucial for us is that all he said in praise of God had become personal to him in his realization of his own and others' need. The gripping message of the psalm for me is that the One who is praised as King of all creation, who is adored in His majesty, grandeur, and goodness, who is acknowledged for His providential care and intervening acts of power, is known and loved personally as He "upholds those who fall."

Only one who had fallen would know that. That's good news for us. When we fall we realize for ourselves that the Lord is gracious and kind. Those two words translate the single Hebrew word hāsîd, *hesed,* which, when used to describe God, refers to that special quality of love He has for His people. That love is God's consistent, indefatigable attitude toward us We are able to experience it to the fullest when we have no other hope or support.

We all trip and stumble at times in our relationships with God, ourselves, and others. We also fail in our calling to live out our faith in the needs of our society. So often we take over the running of our lives and refuse to seek and do God's will. We get into a pattern of independence and miss the power He longs to give us.

Then, when we make a mess of things, we get down on ourselves. We negate the special, unique person we were meant to be. Self-condemnation sets in like a virus. We forget that we are the loved and forgiven sons and daughters of a compassionate Father.

The spillover of that often is a refusal to love ourselves as much as He does, and inevitably, we become negative and critical of others. Judgmentalism is the result of self-justification. Affirming others is difficult when we are out of the flow of God's acceptance of us. We lose our nerve and boldness to live courageously.

Once again we need to fall into the greatness of God. Fear of failure repeats failure. Confession of our failures opens us up to receive the great heart of God filled with compassion, mercy, and goodness. All these attributes of God's nature are revealed in Jesus Christ and sublimely offered to us through the cross. Calvary becomes our solid rock. When we fall, Calvary is our objective source of hope in the midst of our subjective feelings of remorse and self-negation.

Christ's resurrection is our assurance of eternal life and the secret of the abundant life. The same power that raised Jesus from the dead is available to raise us out of the graves of our failures. The risen, reigning Christ, *God with us,* stoops to us when we are beaten and depressed and says, "You are forgiven. Let Me help you back to your feet. Put your hand in Mine. Let Me help you walk and run again."

When we fail and trust in the Lord's unfailing grace, we rediscover that His stature assures our status. When we confessed

Christ as our Lord and Savior, we became a part of His eternal family. There is nothing that can change that. We belong to the Lord now and for eternity.

When we are bowed by the pressures and problems of life, we are blessed with the opportunity of rediscovering and reclaiming our status as saints. A saint is one who is chosen, called, and cherished. We belong to the Lord! The word *saint* does not mean infallible impeccability but the Lord's ownership of us. The root word is *holy*, meaning "to set apart." It does not mean spiritual superiority but that we are holy because we belong to a holy God.

An Absolute Righteousness

The psalmist went on in this magnificent psalm to claim the implications of belonging to the Lord. What does He offer us? Marvel at this:

> The LORD is righteous in all His ways,
> Gracious in all His works.
> The LORD is near to all who call upon Him,
> To all who call upon Him in truth.
> He will fulfill the desire of those who fear Him;
> He also will hear their cry and save them.
> The LORD preserves all who love Him
> But all the wicked He will destroy
> (vv. 17–20).

In times of need we have a fresh experience of the Lord's nature, His nearness, and His newness.

The key biblical word that explains God's nature is *righteousness*. More than just an attribute, it is the source of all His attributes. Righteousness is God's essential character, that which He is, which motivates all that He does. It is the center of His being. Righteousness is His love, out of which He created humankind and gave us the capacity to love Him. Love motivated Him to establish a basis of a right relationship with Him.

He called Israel to be His people and through Moses told them what He desired, "Hear, O Israel: The LORD our God, the LORD is one! You shall love the LORD your God with all your heart, with all your soul, and with all your might" (Deut. 6:4–5).

The Ten Commandments were given as the ethical implementation of love. Putting God first, loving Him in response to His love, was to be the motivation for living all the Commandments. When Israel denied that love and refused to live with love-motivated obedience, God did not wink at the disobedience. His love was expressed in judgment of sin and a way for atonement. God sent His Son into the world—Immanuel, God with us—to provide a cosmic atonement for our sin and an eternal basis for forgiveness.

When we accept that substitutionary sacrifice for our sins, we realize the forgiving love which has been in the Lord's heart for us even before we sinned. We ask for forgiveness because we know that we are already forgiven.

Sin at the base is essentially a refusal to love. All the hurting things we do to ourselves and others are simply because of an unwillingness to receive and express love. When we fall in life, God's love, His righteousness, is our only hope. Just as His love judged sin and forgave it on Calvary, so too the Lord's love confronts us with our failure and then assures us that we are forgiven. He uses our falls creatively to usher us deeper into His grace. There are no lengths to which He will not go to reach us with the assurance that even before we fell, He loved us. Astounding? Yes! The unchangeable righteousness of God, His essential nature of love, catches us when we fall. We fall into greatness.

So we should question how we perceive ourselves. In Jesus Christ we have been brought into a right relationship with God. When we put our trust in Christ we "become the righteousness of God in Him" (2 Cor. 5:21). In Christ we become all that God requires; what we cannot produce ourselves is offered as a free gift. Our status is that we are reconciled, justified, and belong to Him forever in

Christ. This alone gives us courage to begin again after we've fallen
and to pray as we have sung:

> Look, Father, look on His anointed face,
> And only look on us as found in Him;
> Look not on our misusings of Thy grace,
> Our prayer so languid, and our faith so dim:
> For lo! between our sins and their reward
> We set the passion of Thy Son our Lord. [1]

He's Always There

Press on! Consider not only the Lord's nature but also His nearness. He is always there when we call. The psalmist emphasized the
fact that He is near to those who "call upon Him in truth" (v. 18).
That call must be based on what God has told us about His availability, loving forgiveness, and grace; then we are enabled to be
honest about what we have done or has happened to us. We can cry
out for help because we know that nothing will cause the Lord to
leave or forsake us. He endures our neglect, rebellion, misguided
determination to run our own lives, and our unwillingness to trust
Him completely.

So, if we are falling or bowed down by life right now, He not only
is ready to hear and respond to our call, He is the instigator of the
desire to ask for help. The psalm tells us that He saves and loves us.
That means He delivers us and uses the failure as a part of His
strategy for our growth in greatness in the future.

Creative Pardon

Even more remarkably, God loves us as if we had never fallen.
Out of sheer love, He closes the door on the past and opens a new

door for the future. "He will fulfill the desire of those who fear Him" (v. 19).

Here *fear* means awe and wonder, humble receptivity and responsiveness. Out of our falls, He redirects our desires, giving us the courage to ask for what He has planned for us. Failures can be successful if they bring us to want what He wants for us.

Thus we can say with Paul, ". . . one thing I do, forgetting those things which are behind and reaching forward to those things which are ahead, I press toward the goal for the prize of the upward call of God in Christ Jesus" (Phil. 3:13–14). The basis of that lively confidence is what God promised through Jeremiah, fulfilled on the cross, and mediates afresh to us when we fall: ". . . I will forgive their iniquity, and their sin I will remember no more" (Jer. 31:34).

If the Lord doesn't remember or hold the past against us, why should we? He wants to give us the freedom to forgive ourselves as forgiven by Him and forget as completely as He has. If we don't, we will repeat the failure. Life will become a succession of falls not into greatness, but grimness.

Recently at a family camp I was deeply aware of the need of the people to experience the fullness of Christ's indwelling Spirit. So many seemed blocked and lacking a vibrant joy. They were Christians who believed in Christ as Lord and Savior, but many confessed that they were not free.

One morning during the retreat I prayed that the Lord would lead me to just the right passage to preach in the evening service. I needed a word from the Lord for the camp. In my prayers, the word *camp* kept surfacing, so I checked my concordance and reviewed all the passages with the word in them. Deuteronomy 29:11 leaped out at me: "The stranger who is in your camp." The New American Standard Bible renders the phrase the "alien who is within your camp." The Lord had given me what I needed.

The family camp had many aliens and strangers, people who could not give themselves permission to express joy because of failures in the past that made them feel unworthy. They were harboring memories of what they had done or others had done to them. After explaining the context of the Deuteronomy passage about Moses' call for all in the camp of Israel to enter into the covenant which the Lord had made with them, I went on to talk to the self-designated aliens and strangers in our camp. Nothing blocks the outrushing flow of Christ's Spirit from within us as much as unwillingness to love and forgive ourselves as much as He does.

I am thankful that many of those who felt alienated from the Lord, themselves, and the fellowship were set free that night. At the conclusion of the meeting the pastors and elders remained to pray with those who wanted to accept forgiveness and forgive others. They fell from self-righteousness into the greatness of the grace of the Lord, His unmerited, unlimited, unqualified love.

The Guardian of Our Steps

A final word about how falling into the Lord's greatness enables our greatness as His people. Jude promises that the Lord will not only help us when we fall but will keep us from falling:

> Now to Him who is able
> to keep you from stumbling,
> And to present you faultless
> Before the presence of His glory
> with exceeding joy,
> To God our Savior,
> Who alone is wise,
> Be glory and majesty,
> Dominion and power,
> Both now and forever.
> Amen (Jude 24).

How does Christ keep us from stumbling and falling and present us faultless before God? I know of no other way than repeatedly catching us when we do fall so that the memory of that constant help will finally free us to trust Him to guide us in the future. When we fall into His greatness and experience His love, we step more steadily. The Lord conquers our fear of failure. The faultlessness of which Jude spoke is not ours but the Lord's. He presents us faultless because of His forgiveness. Our destination in heaven is sure because of Him. In the meantime, we can press on unafraid, willing to risk in doing His will, living with freedom and joy. Actually, every day He presents us as faultless so that in that day we can dare to live adventurously for Him and with His power.

The fear of failure keeps many of us locked in bondage to our own pride. The fear begins in our early years and grows to be a monster in our minds. Little failures in our childhood or teen years brought judgment and negative responses from parents, teachers, and friends. We became determined to work harder not to fail again, or if we did, to keep it hidden. The success game began. We felt we would be loved and accepted only when we did well. Our own fear of failing made us very stern and angry with others' failures. The result was that they could not be any more honest with us than we were with them. The masks of success were worn to cover up our inner hurts. The repression of our failures made us vulnerable to further failure.

The church is often a part of the syndrome. Grace may be preached, but may not be the ambience of the fellowship. Pretense and artificial piety result. We live two lives: On the outside we project the victorious Christian image, and inside we feel defeated by our lack of consistency between what we believe and what we are.

Our fear of failure is increased by what might happen to people's attitudes toward us if they really knew us. What was said of the people in Nazareth could be said of many churches today. "He (Christ) could do no mighty work there because of their unbelief." Today the unbelief is not about Christ as the Son of God, but about His power to turn our stumbling into stepping stones.

New life comes to those churches that allow people to be honest about their needs and experience grace for past failures and present fears of failing. When pastors and officers of churches are vulnerable about what the Lord has done and is doing in their failures, a sigh of relief is expressed by the congregation. The hiding game is over. Confession in ordered worship becomes much more real. Honesty in small groups is released. The content of teaching in classes becomes more than dull theory and is the Bread of Life for spiritually famished participants. Pious one-upmanship in relationships is replaced by mutual sharing of hurts and hopes. Prayer for each other becomes specific and more personal.

The Spirit of Christ anoints a church like that, and suddenly people realize that He is there to catch them when they fall. Confident in Him, they fall less and risk more. The gospel becomes real, and the people sing for joy. Most of all, the attention is shifted from how good we are (or others ought to be!) to the greatness of the Lord.

I know more of that greatness than I did when I began this study of the Psalms. In addition to meeting the Lord in new ways in the Psalms, I have also discovered a new freedom from the various psalmists whose songs and prayers we have considered. They were open about their needs, quick to confess their sins, and honest about their hopes. They struggled as we do and felt the same disappointments and fears we experience. The power of the Psalms is that they teach us to pray much more honestly. The exuberant bursts of unfettered praise are the result of what the Lord has done in spite of their failures as individuals and as a nation. Therefore, we can come to the Lord just as we are, with the sure knowledge that He won't leave us there. The Psalms teach us how to fall successfully—into the waiting, everlasting arms of God—into His greatness, which by His grace enables our own.

Notes

Chapter 1
1. Artur Weiser, *The Psalms, A Commentary* (London: SLM Press, 1962), 104.

Chapter 2
1. Mitchell Dahood, *The Anchor Bible: Psalms I* (New York: Doubleday, 1965), 48.
2. Leslie Weatherhead, *The Eternal Voice* (Nashville, Tenn.: Abingdon, 1940), 202.
3. From "A Sun-Day Hymn" by Oliver Wendell Holmes.

Chapter 3
1. Charles H. Spurgeon, *The Treasury of David*, unabridg., 2 vols. (Byron Center, Mich.: Associated Publishers and Authors, 1970), 1:246.
2. Herman Melville, *Moby Dick* (New York: Peebles Press International, n.d.), 41.

Chapter 5
1. Thomas Hardy, "Impercipient," *Chief Modern Poets of England and America*, ed. Gerald DeWitt Sanders and John H. Nelson (New York: Macmillan, 1931), 26.

Chapter 8
1. George MacDonald, "What Christ Said," *1000 Quotable Poems*, ed. Thomas Curtis Clark (Chicago: Willet, Clark and Co., 1937), 2.

Chapter 9
1. Source unknown.

Chapter 10
1. Gore Vidal, *The Best Man* (Boston: Little, Brown and Company, 1960), 48–50.
2. From *Cato* by Joseph Addison (1672–1719).

Chapter 11
1. From "Guide Me, O Thou Great Jehovah" by Rev. William Williams.

Chapter 13

1. Samuel Wilberforce, "Just for Today."

2. Sarah K. Bolton, "Live in the Present," *1000 Quotable Poems*, ed. Thomas Curtis Clark (Chicago: Willet, Clark and Co., 1937), 214.

3. J. H. Jowett, *Springs in the Desert, Studies in the Psalms*, (Grand Rapids: Baker, 1976), 211.

4. From "Rabbi ben Esra xxxii" by Robert Browning.

5. Quoted in a sermon by Frank W. Boreham (1871–1959) and reprinted in *Mountains in the Mist* (London: Epworth Press, 1914).

Chapter 15

1. *Calvin's Commentaries*, trans. James Anderson, 22 vols. (Grand Rapids: Baker, 1981), 4:126.

Chapter 16

1. Copyright © 1984, Lloyd John Ogilvie.

Chapter 17

1. F. B. Meyer, *Great Verses Through the Bible* (Grand Rapids: Zondervan, 1972), 238.

Chapter 18

1. From "Aurora Leigh," book vii, by Elizabeth Barrett Browning.

Chapter 19

1. From stanza 2 of the hymn "And Now, O Father, Mindful of the Love" by William Bright.